A Love Affair with India

Mabel Jones and Eunice Jones Mathews

The Story of the Wife and Daughter of E. Stanley Jones

by Martha Gunsalus Chamberlain

A Love Affair with India:
The Story of the Wife and Daughter of E. Stanley Jones

Cover design by Dale Bryant

Published by the General Commission on Archives and History
The United Methodist Church
in cooperation with United Methodist Women and
UMR Communications Inc.

Second printing July 2009

Printed in the United States of America
Printed on acid-free paper

ISBN: 978-1-880927-23-6

DEDICATED

To the glory of God
and to the memory and service of
Mabel Lossing Jones
and in honor of her daughter
Eunice Treffry Jones Mathews,
women of courage and commitment
to the people of India with whom they
share a love affair.

Acknowledgements

Countless resources and unnamed persons deserve profound gratitude, but I expressly acknowledge the following:

Eunice Jones Mathews who generously opened her heart, mind and memory, who shared her writing through the last century, answered unending questions and edited copious manuscripts for factual accuracy and interpretation.

Mabel Lossing Jones, though now deceased, for writing through her hundred-year lifetime and for modeling Christian faith and service.

Anne Mathews Younes and Janice Mathews Stromsen, daughters of Eunice and Jim Mathews and granddaughters of Mabel and E. Stanley Jones, who share the passion of their parents and grandparents.

Bishop James K. Mathews who blessed and encouraged this project.

Sarah Wilke, CEO of UMR Communications Inc., who first affirmed the project enthusiastically and assumed responsibility for publishing and marketing the story.

Robert J. Williams, General Secretary of General Commission on Archives and History of the United Methodist Church, who agreed the story must be published and offered support to underwrite the project.

Amy Forbus at UMR Communications Inc., always available, who managed the complexities of publication.

David McAllister Wilson and James K. Logan, Bishop Susan Morrison, and Harriett Jane Olson, Deputy General Secretary of Women's Division, General Board of Global Ministries, who read and critiqued the manuscript and endorsed its publication.

Louise Duffy, friend of the Mathews family, who graciously commended the book.

Others who helped in a variety of supportive ways, including Jane Ives and Bishop Clifton Ives who shared reports of their India sojourn; Joanne Reich, UMC deaconess; Don Reasoner, translator for GBGM; and certainly Nancy Davis, angel unaware—but God and the Mathewses understand.

My children, including son Russell Chamberlain who read an early draft and guided me with the right questions; my daughters Marcia and Sharon who make me think I can write and accept no excuses; our foster daughter Pam who exudes encouragement.

Ray, my bishop-husband of nearly fifty years, who assumes total responsibility since his retirement for house/yard/cooking/cleaning to provide me that elusive "time to write" that plagues writers—and who totally believes in me, no matter how many years it takes.

All the primary and secondary sources, listed elsewhere, without which the book could not have been written.

I owe a special debt of gratitude to India, extraordinary land and warm-hearted people.

This publication is made possible through the gift of Frederick E. Maser and Mary Louise Jarden Maser.

Contents

Prologue

In years to come, tell your children about it . . .
pass the story down from generation to generation.
—Joel 1:3

Soon after the turn of the twentieth century, Mabel Lossing sailed to a life-changing destination: India. Destined to become the wife of E. Stanley Jones and give birth to Eunice, their only child, she would initiate innovation as an educator extraordinaire.

More than thirty years earlier in 1869, two other courageous Methodist women had climbed the gangplank together onto an ocean steamer that likewise carried them to India. Isabella Thoburn, sister of Methodist Bishop James Thoburn, would develop the first women's college in all of Asia, while Clara Swain, M.D. built the first hospital for women in Asia.

Young and remarkably independent, this triad gave themselves to India, each convinced of God's calling to this "jewel in the crown" of British colonialism. Undoubtedly, God was already there. Their passionate, unquenchable fire ignited generations of Indian women, children and men, while the Methodist Church in India owes much of its growth to these women and others like them.

The zenith of powerful, confident and beautiful womanhood, Eunice Jones Mathews, like her mother, admits her humble dependence both on her God and on those courageous, determined women who built the bridges she and her mother crossed into meaningful service. Her story begins in the middle of a scenario, because exploring any epoch invariably traces its roots into the unfathomable influence of a Past.

The cultural norm of "women's work for women" for this cohort restricted choices and limited opportunities in the nineteenth and early twentieth centuries. Yet this dynamic duo rendered their service to God and humankind in extraordinary venues, continuing to impact thousands today. While the result is good, losing the untold story of more than a century of their Christian mission would be tragic.

Volumes about the life and times, the theology and missiology of E. Stanley Jones line the library shelves of Christians worldwide, but something is missing. Rather than an adjunct to one of the most famous and renowned missionaries of the twentieth century, Mabel Lossing Jones is herself one of the most accomplished—yet little known—Methodist missionaries, having served forty-two years in India, accomplishing miraculous feats through prayer and ingenuity.

Mabel Jones also reared their daughter Eunice who is defined neither by her celebrated father nor by her eminent United Methodist bishop-husband. Her own unsung contributions to mission and ministry Eunice tenaciously hides from public accolades. To know her is to respect and love her. One stands in awe of these two women who defy stereotypes.

Eunice respects her mother Mabel to the extent that this book nearly aborted in its early gestation. "My mother"—Eunice insists—"she is the one whose story must be told. She is the hero, the extraordinary one." Further conversation to persuade her to write her autobiography invoked this amused response: "Oh no . . . there's nothing to tell. I want you to write about my mother."

Now, the gentle giant Eunice Jones Mathews walks into the twenty-first century in the presence of her mother Mabel's spirit. Spanning three centuries, they forge link after link of the story. Narratives from Mabel Lossing Jones' prolific writing and Eunice's razor-sharp memory and writings provide the backdrop. But the story of their contributions to the great century of Christian mission in India and globally hangs in the air like a balloon ready to burst, forever unrealized and unnoticed unless somehow captured in written narrative.

* * * * *

In 2003 Eunice Jones Mathews returned to the land she loves, to

Sitapur, India. This time with her husband and daughters, she wanted the family to hear her still vivid memories of the night sounds in her "circle" of life at the mission. As a child on warm moonlit nights in Sitapur, Eunice had slept on the roof in her mosquito net tent and read to her heart's content while the night sounds kept her company.

In the civil lines each house had a watchman who patrolled the yard. Every night, the chant began at the deputy commissioner's property as one watchman called out in ***Hindustani***, "Keep awake! Keep awake! Midnight is coming and the thieves will be here!" The watchman at the next house picked up the mantra, "Keep awake! Keep awake! Midnight is coming . . ." To Eunice's listening ears the call ebbed and flowed around the circle until it lulled her to sleep.

The monkeys voiced another theme in the night chorus in the circle. Considered sacred by the ***Hindus***, they were never killed. Hordes of red-bottomed monkeys played wild nocturnal games, while one watchman did nothing but chase monkeys, calling out, "I'm chasing my monkeys!" On and on they circled through the night.

Music often drifted around the circle from a wedding in the bazaar. Mostly retirees from the British-India Army band, they always played the same ditties, Scottish melodies, British tunes, and even "The Bear Went over the Mountain" repeated dozens of times, while firecrackers punctuated the darkness.

The Joneses tried to remember to tell their guests that packs of jackals invaded the circle at night. The lead jackal called out what sounded like, "I smell the blood of a dead human," followed by the others braying, "Where, where, where . . .?" When shaky visitors inquired about the spooky braying, young Eunice relished her own nonchalant assurance, "Oh, that's just our jackals!"

A sudden harsh jangle often interjected the night sounds. To protect the fruit in the Company Gardens next door to the mission, watchmen put stones in tin cans and hung them on the fruit trees with ropes that they jiggled intermittently to frighten away the flying foxes, a bat species.

Eunice recounts that return trip that now lives only in her memory. “The night noises are gone!” she cries out forlornly. “The green, grassy oval with a road running around it has disappeared. In place of bungalows, small houses have sprung up as tenements. Ruined! I cannot find my wonderful place. My circle is gone!”

* * * * *

Eunice’s little circle may be gone, but the work continues in an ever-expanding circle wider than the human eye can see, a miracle her mother—with all her faith—never dreamed possible. Having just celebrated 150 years of Methodism on the subcontinent, and the 25th year of autonomy, the church and the Mabel Jones Boys School continue to change lives with the Gospel message.

The Mathews family had planned to participate in this grand celebration at Isabella Thoburn College in ***Lucknow***, and were greatly disappointed to be unable to attend. Representing them, United Methodist Bishop Clifton Ives and Ms. Jane Ives in 2006 rejoiced to watch the assembly processing through the streets of Lucknow. With banners and flags flying, the parade witnessed to their faith with a huge cross and joyful singing—all included in the greater circle.

A few months earlier, with their son Stan and his wife Patti, Eunice Jones Mathews and husband Jim Mathews “walked the boundaries” of Mabel Jones’s home place where she had grown into the extraordinary woman she became. A Hindu custom, the father walks the property boundaries with his son—but more than that—shows the son his place in the great scheme of things, where hearth and earth, and past and present meld with future. Otherwise, these entities would soon become terra incognita. So, they walked in the footsteps of Mabel and Eunice’s ancestors in Clayton, Iowa, bordering the great Mississippi.

“Walking the boundaries” is reminiscent of the celebration of the Passover by the Jewish people. Today as part of their ritual for thousands of years, fulfilling the Old Testament mandate the children still ask: Why do you do this? And the father answers with clarity: This reminds us that the Lord brought us out of Egypt with great power . . .

Likewise, when Christians celebrate the sacrament of Holy Communion, they continue the centuries-old tradition initiated by Jesus at his last earthly Passover meal: "When you do this, do it in remembrance . . ." Each storyteller passes it on while "walking the boundaries" with the next generation.

Driving on to Colorado, the family reveled in the extravagant beauty surrounding them. Little did the Mathews family realize the significance of "walking the boundaries" together on that day in Iowa. But they clearly understood that the story lives on. In Boulder, Colorado, the path diverged, as Jim suffered a stroke.

Yet, the story continues. Shaken on hearing this news about Jim, I knew the narrative had to take the shape of the written word—quickly. Now it is my turn, my privilege to pass it on. The value of the oral tradition requires that the storyteller pass on what she knows—one way or another in this technological era. Survival depends on it.

Mabel and Eunice Jones Mathews have forged their links. Not only found in the archives of the United Methodist Church, but also in the lives of generations now touching three centuries, the story of this duo continues in the Mathews's three children, their six grandchildren and now two great, great grandchildren of Mabel and E. Stanley Jones.

They and their progeny understand the vital link of the ***griot***. In the oral tradition, the revered African griot memorizes the village history and stories of his people. He tells the stories repeatedly, providing the foundation on which the future builds. When the storyteller dies, the village mourns deeply, for it is as though a great library has burned to the ground.

Eunice Jones Mathews personifies the griot, continuing to shape and provide substance to this story. The griot lives!

Read on . . .

—Martha Gunsalus Chamberlain

Chapter 1

A Divine Plan

Messages from the desk of God come through the stories of our fellow human beings. We only need to listen.
—Desmond Tutu

The cacophony of hundreds of blackbirds perched in the ***neem trees*** called Mabel Lossing Jones from her misty dream in the rising April heat. She stretched one hand toward her husband, and then remembered. Stanley was not there. He would return soon—a word that poses a fluid meaning in exotic lands. She considered whether the usual alarm of raucous crows or an already fading dream—or something extraordinary—had awakened her.

Mabel propped herself on one elbow and peered through the mosquito net tucked in snugly on all sides of her bed. Carefully loosening the edges, she struggled to roll over and sit upright on the edge of the ***nawar***. An Indian had woven the rough, two-inch width cotton tapes onto the bed frame, while another removed the seeds from the ceiba tree and fluffed the silken mass that wraps the seeds to fashion a soft kapok mattress for their marriage bed.

That's when she felt it again: a band of contracting muscle tightened across the fullness of her lower torso. Clutching her bulging belly with both hands, she was convinced: A tiny boy or girl would surely suckle her full breasts by nightfall. If only Stanley would arrive to welcome their creation on this day. But a forceful kick was the only response to her musing, and she arose to splash tepid water from the basin on her face.

Already the eastern horizon shimmered with the golds and reds of another hot day at the Methodist Mission in Sitapur, India, where a thermometer would be a superfluous luxury. The mercury might burst through the glass as the temperature sometimes climbed above 120 degrees Fahrenheit. The temperature made little difference in choosing from her limited wardrobe. Mabel's simple, modest clothes still suffocated her in April and proved neither protective during the monsoons nor adequately comfortable during cold winter days.

She ached to climb to the rooftop and lose herself in the magnificent few moments of a new day's dawning. But she'd promised Stanley that in this last month of pregnancy she would not take such chances.

* * * * *

A sudden powerful flashback that strengthened her faith each time it appeared reminded Mabel of the miracle and mystery of God at work. Like the burning bush for Moses and a long-ago conversation for herself, the symbolism had one meaning: God was in it. Mabel pictured her discussion with a woman from India ten years earlier following her stories about the needs in India. About to graduate from Upper Iowa University, Mabel had thanked her perfunctorily. But she'd found the woman so fascinating, so challenging that she began to ask questions.

Then the speaker surprised Mabel with her own questions. "What are your plans after you graduate?"

"Oh, I plan to teach," she replied, "probably at home."

"Dozens of people here could take your place. Have you thought about going to India to teach?"

"Well . . . no . . ." Mabel replied.

The woman from India had erected a signpost at the crossroad and pounded it deep into the tender soil. Mabel considered the choice that was hers; but the plan was God's. Once in that exotic place, she hardly equated her present state with any thought that she had chosen her life's passion. Rather, this place, this work had chosen her. Surely God was in it. An old adage says: If God calls me to be a missionary, I would not stoop to be a king.

That Mabel had arrived in India at all was a direct result of what happened at the Tremont Street Methodist Episcopal Church in Boston. Resolute women hacked through tradition and resistance to change the trajectory of male dominance that controlled all funds, including large amounts raised by women for the General Mission Board. In spite of the male "spy" sent to observe and deter their activity, the indomitable women had formed the Woman's Foreign Missionary Society (WFMS) in March 1869.

Determined to act, one passionate woman cried out: "Shall we lose [our first missionary] because we have not the needed money? No, rather let us walk the streets of Boston in our calico robes and save the expense of more costly apparel . . . I move the appointment of Miss Thoburn as our missionary to India."

No longer raising money for the General Mission Board to allocate, the WFMS recruited and supported their first two missionaries, two women who sailed together on November 3, 1869, for India. Isabella Thoburn established the first university for women in Asia. The second missionary, medical doctor Clara Swain founded the first hospital for women in Asia in 1870.

Thirty-five years later in 1904, in that same Tremont Street Church in Boston, the WFMS commissioned Mabel Lossing, and she sailed for India as an education missionary.

Women's mission societies evolved along with the division/uniting of the people called Methodists. Women's work thrived, both in the United States and globally. In one village church in South India, the Christian outcaste/untouchable women impacted community social needs to the extent that the non-Christian women envied them. So, they organized the first and only Hindu Women's Society for Christian Service!

In fact, in 1906 Bishop J.M. Thoburn, brother of Isabella Thoburn, wrote an article that expressed both support and admiration for the women who changed the face of Methodist missions. "The achievements of our missionary women have been the most striking features of the work . . . they have a more wonderful story to rehearse than have their brethren."

In spite of the declaration of the General Mission Board that " . . . women should retain their old-time unobtrusiveness and not assert their personalities, other than social obligations, and remain in their sheltered homes," they had ignited a fire that would not be extinguished.

E. Stanley Jones arrived in India in 1907, appointed by the Methodist General Board of Mission. Although he had studied law in Baltimore, much to his father's consternation he chose to contribute in ways more meaningful to him—perhaps in India or China. India it would be.

While Stanley served the English-speaking ***Lal Bagh*** Methodist Church in Lucknow, Mabel had been sent to fill in at the Lal Bagh Teacher Training School, later named for Isabella Thoburn, in the same city. Mabel also played the organ at the church for about a year without ever meeting the young preacher. Until—one day he approached her in the aisle of his church. James Robb wrote that Stanley Jones "wasn't quite sure how to proceed with romance." According to the superintendent of the Jabbulpore School, he blurted out a stumbling proposal, asking her to be his wife.

And so it was that Mabel found herself ready to deliver their baby in India. She had watched God work the plan that stretched over her lifetime like a canopy. This day would be no different.

* * * * *

A deafening silence descended on the compound as the blackbirds took flight with a sudden, flapping whoosh until nightfall beckoned them again to settle in the neem and ***banyan trees***. Mabel heard the servants; she and Stanley preferred to call them "helpers." It was the rich, the English, the military cantonment who had "servants."

Mabel's American friends envied her, but little could they even imagine the complexities of living in India in 1914. Had Mabel Jones done all her own housework, she would have done nothing else. "I might as well stay at home to do housework," she wrote to a friend. "I have other work here."

While most Western women managed their own households, the women in Sitapur, India, had neither electricity nor running water. Added to this was the complexity of the caste system that strictly delegates duties to specific persons—for life. For one Indian to perform all the household duties was impossible, because each had his explicit duty; lines could not be crossed.

As the Christian family was "unclean" to a Hindu who would never have handled their food, the Jones's cook Bhulan was a ***Muslim***. An enviable baker, he inverted a dishpan over the charcoal embers for an oven. Charcoal was the usual source of fuel, as wood was expensive. The kitchen was housed in a separate building away from the house.

The houseboy—boy indicating the British word for a servant rather than age of the man—was responsible for running the daily routine, supervising all other helpers. The water boy and sweepers, inexorably imprisoned in their caste, belonged on the lowest rung of the social ladder.

Although castes are now outlawed, the social stratum into which one is born still shapes the identity of every Indian. While many castes and sub-groups have evolved, the complex hierarchical system includes ***Brahmins***, the highest class with knowledge and power, such as priests, scholars and teachers; the ***Kshatriyas***, comprised of the warriors; the ***Vaishyas*** with its merchants and landowners. The ***Shudras*** are the fourth of the primary castes, whose livelihood depends on the upper class, and whose purpose is to serve them well. The ***Dalits***, regarded as so far beneath other Indians that these "untouchables" are not even included among the four major castes, are called scavengers, so designated by society as dung. They could no more cross over into a higher caste than a cow could become human, but—***Mahatma*** Gandhi coined a word describing them as ***Harijans***, children of God.

At the mission every three to five hours, the Dalit sweeper made the rounds of all the toilets to empty human waste from the pots into the cart he pushed every day of his adult life. These toilets could be described as adult potty chairs, with a wood seat and pot beneath it. For obvious reasons, it is said that the sweeper knew before anyone else when a birth was imminent. Still another man cleaned the floors and the courtyard, while yet another carried water in the pigskin container, the ultimate defilement for both Hindu and Muslim.

Guards from among the Dalits were purported to be the best, because other thieves avoided such a household. After all, they were "eating your salt" was the explanation. A North American might say, You don't bite the hand that feeds you. A missionary who moved into the mission house temporarily was aghast when he heard Mabel had hired one from the thief caste. "I'll never hire a watchman from the thief caste," he ranted. "Besides, he's a Hindu! I'll hire a Christian!"

"Go ahead," Mabel told the new missionary, "but I think you'd be wise to hire one." Some months later, he awoke from a night of sleep on the roof where everyone slept to catch the evening breezes. He descended the steps to discover an emptied house. Finding the Christian night watchman asleep on the verandah, he questioned him, "Where's my furniture? Where is everything?"

Together they searched the premises. On the tennis court adjoining the house, they found all of his property. The watchman had apparently been chloroformed into a stupor. Nothing was stolen, and the lesson was well-taught and well-learned.

Many Indian communities, the government and social agencies to this day devise both overt and covert means to break down such discrimination among castes. Physician Maybelle Arole in ***Jamkhed***, Maharashtra, arranged children waiting for care into groups based on the color of clothes they wore rather than by caste distinctions. Again, rather than the customary separation according to caste, when the village health workers arrived for training, representing all the castes, she provided one giant blanket under which they all slept. As part of their training, Dr. Arole showed them bone x-rays from each caste and their own blood samples to be examined microscopically, instructing them to identify differences among castes. Of course, they could find none.

Dr. Arole wisely built a well within the separate confines of the Dalits. The women from the upper castes were welcome to draw the same water, or they could walk many more miles to the next nearest water source to obtain unclean water.

But the Indians were not the only ones who organized life around a hierarchical system. The British officials perpetuated, and in fact, instituted further stratification during colonial rule. India continued the same level of officialdom and placed its stamp of approval on government hierarchy. Each state had its governor, a deputy commissioner, a civil surgeon, and the superintendent of police—always all British. They trained young Indian men to work under the official tutelage of the British until eventually some were permitted to replace some British in the Indian Civil Service (ICS).

Slightly lower were persons who were not in government or ICS, such as heads of important organizations or companies. All tradespeople and other assorted Brits were considered "***boxwallas***." Likewise, the British counted missionaries—at least advantaged along with the Brits as being Caucasian—as belonging to this group, though of slightly lower status.

* * * * *

Suddenly a new contraction gripped Mabel, creeping around her torso into the lumbar region. Squatting on the chamber pot, she noted new signs that signaled the descent of the baby. Yes, this was more than a fetus, more than a pregnancy. Her baby pushed into the birth canal with pure intention.

"Mmmmm," she groaned quietly. She wondered if it were time to call the Swedish nurse who would attend her delivery. As the pain abated, Mabel began planning her daily tasks. This being her first, surely the baby wouldn't arrive for many more hours—that she knew. She planned extravagantly for a busy day's activity until a momentary wave of nausea and panic gripped her. Neither fear nor pain had ever intimidated her purposes, but suddenly her solitude in the midst of a bustling household was as palpable as her full abdomen. There was no delegating this duty.

She reminded herself that women have babies every day. Most live through it. She pushed aside nagging questions about birthing a normal baby. If only Stanley could . . . but another contraction pushed that thought off track.

Mabel heard Bhulan talking with the milkman who arrived each morning with cow and calf in tow. He milked the cow on the spot, filling a container with as much as was needed for that day. The milkman believed his cow gave more milk if her calf were present, so he placed the calf in front of his cow or, if she no longer had a calf, he propped up a stuffed surrogate nearby.

Long before the blackbirds stirred, the ***bhisti*** had already drawn water. That was his only task, all day long, with the help of two oxen that pulled the pigskin leather water bag up the incline from the house to the well and back again. Then the bhisti, or water carrier, filled the containers in all the rooms of the house. Mabel had grown accustomed to its pinkish cast from the potassium permanganate thrown regularly into the deep well to kill dangerous microorganisms.

"That's my next big project," she thought. She planned to build a superior system called the Persian water wheel about which she had read. Ox-power rather than hydro-power submerges each attached bucket that surfaces brimming with water. Eventually, she would also build a septic system about which she had read. But today they depended on the sweeper and the muscular bhisti. He filled the bag and guided the oxen pulling the bulging leather bag to the house. They would need plenty of water that Mabel knew was somehow connected to birthing a baby. At that moment she needed a drink of hot tea, but the thought of food repulsed her.

In the grip of a new contraction she inadvertently moaned, "Ohhhhhh."

"What is it, ***Memsahib***?" Bhulan cried out. The strict Muslim would never invade her privacy, but his anxiety poured through the cracks and over the walls with their openings at the top for air circulation. He felt curiously responsible with the ***sahib*** away from home. This American woman was strong and brave and independent—but the birth of a baby was imminent.

Ten years earlier, Mabel Lossing had chosen God's plan for her life. Now, at the age of thirty-four, Mabel Jones prepared to deliver her baby, separated by oceans and ten thousand miles from family, and even from her husband engaged in God's "other" work. Her thoughts wandered until finally, the pangs of childbirth eradicated all thoughts of past or future or God or Stanley—working its power throughout Mabel's whole being. The demands of both body and soul eclipsed all else. She laid aside her quill pen. She relinquished earlier plans for her day's work. She breathed deeply. Nothing else mattered. Once more, the plan was God's. She would deliver her baby—in India.

On the other side of the wall that separated Mabel's bedroom from the huge verandah of the imposing structure, the ***coolie*** was particularly engaged with his work to cool the main rooms of the large house. While shopping in the bazaar, Mabel had found the man and his wife, both blind, begging. With their son who was both deaf and mute, the family served the household faithfully for the next twenty-one years. The formerly low-caste blind beggar who, with his family, eventually became Christian, had the perfect job.

By means of a rope stretched through a hole in the wall to a ***punkah***, a long plank with a three-foot canvas tacked to the bottom, the coolie moved the canvas back and forth to create movement of air. Sometimes overcome with the afternoon heat, he tied the rope to his toes and snoozed, waking suddenly to yank the rope as his own body heat became uncomfortable. But on this day the low conversation and bustling inside quickened his movements. The bhisti periodically joined him on the verandah to drench the woven bamboo screens on the tall doorframes to further the illusion of air conditioning.

Through the interminably long day, the heat and pain crawled to the finish line. Outside the bedroom of the memsahib, the workers assumed forced nonchalance as they carried out their work. Respect—whether or not they understood her ways—trumped their questions about Mabel Jones. Without exception, they wished her well.

Inside her bedroom, boiled water, stacks of neatly folded, clean rags, crude instruments to cut the cord, an empty bucket for the placenta—it was all there, except for analgesic relief. The trained Indian doctor in the bazaar section could have come to assist, but he had never examined a woman patient without a cloth between the woman and her doctor. Mabel did not want to accept that decorum on this day.

The Swedish missionary nurse friend who would attend the birth was a "faith missionary," sent by her denomination to serve while trusting God—not God through the church—to support her. Mabel discovered one such missionary in the bazaar starving until Mabel rescued her. Meager perhaps, but fifty dollars a month was pledged by the women in Mabel's home church in Iowa who each gave two dollars monthly to support her work. At least she felt connection through their financial gifts borne on wings of prayer.

Relieved as she was to welcome her midwife, Mabel's anxiety increased as the hours wore on. Would it never end? As temperatures soared, the nurse's anxiety also thickened with the heavy air. She longed to cut a hole in the oppressive heat so her exhausted patient could breathe deeply between the pains and the panting. The bedclothes were soaked with the perspiration of hard labor and body fluids. Something was not right. Something did not appear normal to the experienced nurse. To lose this baby would be tragic enough, but Mabel's life was also at stake.

Finally, in desperation she sent a servant to find the British civil surgeon. At last the very young man, fresh-faced and eager, just out from England with his new medical degree, arrived for his first delivery in India. The nurse had to ask him to repeat his name; then, assured she had heard correctly, the nurse swallowed hard and chose to sidestep any introduction to Mabel—for good reason.

His name: T.B. Butcher.

Chapter 2

Straining Soup in Sitapur

When all the rooms of the house fill with smoke,
it's not enough to say an angel is sleeping on the chimney.
—Gregory Orr

Both Muslim and Hindu workers hardly dared to breathe. Gathered around the courtyard outside the drama in the bedroom, they waited to hear the first cry of the infant. The day was long and hot. They watched the Swedish nurse enter Mabel's bedroom. More soft cloths and boiled water—always a staple for home births—were passed through the doorway into the hands of the nurse. No cries from either mother or child pierced the morning stillness or sultry afternoon. By evening, each servant and attendant prayed to the Almighty God and a host of lesser gods that Memsahib would at least live—child or not.

God's plan prevailed. Although Stanley did not appear, at least

Dr. Butcher did, and he lived up to his name. Mother and the girl child survived, although that other children did not follow is hardly surprising. Young Dr. Butcher seemed as pleased and relieved as the new mother, whom he left with years of unnecessary misery from his botched attempts. Their bodies seemingly all in one piece after their treacherous birth journey together, mother and child continued on their miraculous path, growing in grace and favor to bless the world—a dynamic duo indeed.

Gathering what little strength remained, Mabel lifted the tiny, red infant to her breast. In spite of blood and water, mucus and meconium, an instinctual and spiritual connection flooded every cell of her being with powerful love for her baby. This child of India began her earthly journey on April 29, 1914, and would for the next century be at home in the global village.

When Stanley arrived to welcome his new baby daughter, they bonded for a lifetime of close camaraderie in spite of months—and sometimes years—of physical separation. Decades later, at age one hundred, Mabel responded thoughtfully to a question about her happiest memory: "The day Stanley came home after Eunice's birth and held me in his arms," she quietly murmured.

* * * * *

Eunice was born into British India. The extraordinary history and culture of India far exceeded any advantages introduced by the British. As far back as the Buddhist Emperor Ashoka, after violent beginnings in the third century B.C.E., his edicts promoted the rights of all, while Aristotle denied freedom to women and slaves. Some 1800 years later, the Muslim emperor Akbar proclaimed that "no man should be interfered with on account of religion," while Catholics in Europe were persecuting Jews with the inquisition and burning heretics at the stake.

Early Moghul history boasts riches of art and architecture such as the ***Taj Mahal***, the sight of which even today demands veneration. Its emperors claimed multiple wives, such as Akbar's harem numbering three hundred, each of whom wore a small mirror on her right thumb to monitor her appearance. Literate and self-possessed, they were carried about on ***palaquins*** carried by four to six men.

Following a six-month voyage, Sir Thomas Roe arrived in India in 1615 and requested the initiation of a trade route on behalf of King James of England. It is hardly surprising that Europeans such as the Dutch and Portuguese, in addition to the British, had for centuries vied for control of India's spice route that developed into much more than spices. Pirates like William Kidd pursued less diplomatic approaches to procuring the riches of the subcontinent, capturing ships bearing pepper and ***cardamom***, saltpeter, liquor, tobacco, coffee, tea and textiles.

India's textiles have inspired exotic descriptions. Cotton muslins were called "evening dew," and woven yarns were portrayed as "the web of the woven wind." In ***Kashmir***, finely woven shawls were made from the inner fleece of a rare mountain goat, and the artisans' hand-painted chintz shone with brilliant colors, yet were washable. These Indian beauties were so in demand that one writer complained that "Europe bleedeth to enrich Asia."

But gradually in the nineteenth century, the British began to treat both Muslim and Hindu Indians as "low class." Unconscionable racism explicit in British imperialism in India in the nineteenth and into the twentieth centuries is illustrated by Viceroy Lord Mayo: "We are British gentlemen engaged in the magnificent work of governing an inferior race."

By the 20th century, of 300 million people in India, 234 million answered to the British Raj. Although the British controlled India through their East India Trade Company for more than a century, it was not until the mutiny of 1857 that the Crown took over the whole sub-continent, allowing the more than five hundred native states in India of varying sizes to function more or less independently, but always under their watchful eye.

The 1857 rebellion would not be the first attempt to sever the bondage that, on the surface, appeared to benefit the Indian people.

Not unlike the Indian caste system, the British—even in that country not their own—arrogantly relegated citizens to classes of servitude. Although both British and Indians suffered casualties, the Indians suffered the greatest losses. *The Bombay Telegraph* reported many of the atrocities that today would be designated as war crimes, such as adopting the policy of no prisoners, preferring instead to blow mutineers from cannons, or lining up prisoners and shooting all simultaneously, killing whole villages of children, women and men suspected of being sympathetic to the rebel cause.

Following the fall of Delhi, a letter from General Montgomery to Captain Hodson shows approval of the massacres by high-ranking officers: "All honour [sic] to you for catching the king and slaying his sons. I hope you will bag many more!" The British press reported that all the residents within the walls of Delhi were bayoneted on the spot. They were not mutineers, but residents of the city who "trusted to our well-known mild rule for pardon. I am glad to say they were disappointed," wrote Montgomery with unfeeling rancor.

Captain Hodson also confessed that in spite of his love for the army, the conduct of professed Christians was one of the most humiliating facts connected with the siege. Christians of any nationality at war humiliate the name they bear. Describing the coalescing forces that revolted against the British Raj, Thomas Lowe wrote that ". . . the cow-killer and the cow-worshipper, the pig hater and the pig-eater had revolted together," resulting in an estimated death toll in the hundreds of thousands.

*****

While these events preceded the days of Mabel's work, she was well aware of the wars that overshadowed her arrival in India and rumors of wars to come in the twentieth century. But fortunately her view was limited as to the influence of this warring disease that infected humankind and would directly impact her and Stanley and Eunice.

So it was that within days of Eunice's birth, mother Mabel resumed her meticulous planning for the school that she was sent to rescue. Already experienced in administration and teaching, Mabel had first served in Khandwa in central India where she became the sole administrator of the orphanage and was also one of only two teachers. Among her tasks was to search the streets for abandoned children, including babies who lay beside or on top of their dead mothers, victims of famine. At the same time Mabel was honing her skills as fundraiser and innovator. Nor was begging beneath her in her early career as she pleaded for a medical missionary. The only doctor available was a ***Parsee*** who would not himself tend to the girls, but sent instead an ill-equipped assistant when called.

During that time, Mabel also completed her master's degree from Upper Iowa University in 1906, even as she studied and practiced the Hindi language four hours a day. She eventually also learned ***Urdu***, ***Sanskrit*** and German, and studied classical languages including Greek and Latin. Mabel bemoaned the insufficient number of hours in the day, and wrote this psalm of lament in a newsletter:

"Oh Life! Why dost thou leave so little time to live? That is what I feel like saying at the end of each day. And sometimes I say, God, please forgive me for rushing past those lovely roses on the way to school, for not stopping [for] the fragrance of jasmine, for not answering these letters from friends and relatives who are so good to me. God has given us so much that is lovely and beautiful! I wonder if [God] is entirely pleased that we give so little time to appreciate those gifts. But God knows that it is love for Him and His needy children that sends us to them with so little time to spare."

During her days at Khandwa, Mabel wrote what became her mantra throughout her years in India: "If only I could do without the servants." While they spared her the work of running a household in what today would be considered intolerable circumstances, they also occupied much of her time in teaching, training, organizing—and exasperation.

One incident counts as metaphor for the ongoing experiences that Mabel, too, strained through less than palatable filters to hang on to sanity and commitment in difficult circumstances. She had just completed eating her soup when the children's ***ayah*** reported, "One of the baby's napkins [diapers] is missing that the ***dhobi*** has not returned."

So, Mabel called the dhobi and he said that the cook had borrowed the napkin to strain the soup. "I called the cook," Mabel wrote, "and he said 'yes,' because I was so busy in the school that he did not want to disturb me to find a cloth—and I suppose they are wondering why I made such a fuss!"

When news of Mabel's extraordinary administrative ability and gifted teaching continued to spread, she was sent to Jabulpur to start a teacher training school, still in existence and called ***Havabagh***, meaning "fresh air." As her fame filtered among educators, she was next sent to Lucknow where she started their teacher training school that later was incorporated into the Isabella Thoburn University for women, where Mabel also taught and was appointed to its Board of Governors.

In the early days of the university, a conversation between Isabella and a Hindu gentleman whom Thoburn had met in Lucknow shows the resistance to equal opportunities for women. The man had several daughters, so Thoburn asked him to send them to her school. He responded disdainfully, "My daughters? I would just as soon send you my cow for all the good it would do." Few Indian women in that cohort were taught to read because of their "defective intellectual powers." Even as women and slaves in the United States were denied education and civil liberties, so it was in India.

* * * * *

Sent in 1912 to Sitapur to three schools in disrepair, both physically and academically, Mabel and Stanley at first worked together. Preacher, writer—yes—but Stanley was no educator, and as he moved fully into his call to evangelism, Mabel Jones strode confidently into her own calling.

The area was called the United Provinces. At the Methodist boarding school that included an orphanage for forty-five boys on the mission, plus two city schools with a hundred and fifty non-Christian boys in the city, Mabel broke ground, both literally and figuratively.

First of all, no one in India had heard of a female "headmaster" for a boys' boarding school, or of women teaching boys, or of a Caucasian serving on the municipal council of a city. But to raving accolades, Mabel served twenty years as the twenty-first person on the Sitapur Municipal Council—the only female, the only non-Indian, the only American, and certainly the only Christian to have served the evenly divided Muslim/Hindu council.

While Mabel recognized she could not change centuries-old protocol quickly, she also determined to find ways to execute excellence in education. Biding her time, the opportunity arrived simply enough. When the male teacher for the kindergarten boys became ill, Mabel needed to replace him.

"Let your wife take the class," she told the ailing teacher.

Never! The townspeople would be outraged for a woman to teach their boys!"

Well, I don't have time to find another male teacher right now, so your wife will have to do it."

At the end of the term, Mabel wisely told the woman teacher to move up a grade to continue teaching the same class. Then she appointed another female to teach the kindergarten, and so on, continuing the plan year after year until all women teachers taught the children. After the initial uproar, all realized that the boys had learned more than those in any other school, and after six or seven years, they could not refute the spectacular result. Soon, those at the mission school were completing their work in half the customary time, resulting in twice as many boys attending.

From disaster to extraordinary success, the school proved

Mabel's approach was wise. Some ignored, but most praised the new system whose students excelled in government exams with scores above all others. As one of the first schools in north India that accepted women teaching boys, the success in Sitapur also emphasized the benefit of introducing respect for women to male students. A vital part of Mabel's curriculum included teacher training, so their excellence was not surprising.

The passage of time told the rest of the story. Having arrived at the mission school as "jungly [sic] little pieces of humanity, who did not know how to wear a pair of pants," as Mabel once described some of her boys, they became successful, contributing members of society—some Christian, some Hindu and some Muslim. One became a Methodist bishop. Where children could not go to them, teachers such as Sundar Singh held five to six schools a day in different locations, using as his only textbook, The Gospel of St. John. Masih Dayal, son of a considered ignorant and low-caste coolie, became pastor of a prominent church in ***Bombay***, and Claudius Ram served as doctor to a large community.

In 1919 Mabel reported to the North India Conference: The seven women teachers, in classrooms five hours a day, also have responsibilities in the hostel for the boarding students. A visiting government official reportedly said that Sitapur is the school "beyond criticism. If that is true," he said, "it must be run by women, for I have yet to find a model boys' school under men!" They learned respect for women and for one another regardless of caste, as well as self-reliance and exemplary moral behavior in an atmosphere of joyful learning.

In addition to teaching, part of Mabel's dream had been to become a journalist. Having already been published in American magazines such as *Harpers* and *The Atlantic Monthly*, Mabel continued to write, but under a pen name so that she would not compete in any way with her husband, already recognized for his writing. Years later when Eunice saw a check arrive from a major American magazine, Eunice recalls begging her mother to reveal her pen name, but the modest educator/linguist/writer replied, "I'll take that secret to my grave." So she did.

No one can dispute the impact of Mabel Jones's writing, whether to unnamed magazines, or to the *Women's Missionary Friend* or the *Junior Missionary Friend* to connect young Methodist readers in the States with life on foreign soil in the name of the church. In one such newsletter Mabel wrote about thirty to forty children chasing after a woman's carriage, crying out for her to give them a Sunday school about which they had heard. The woman did stop, and in minutes seventy children gathered around her, standing in the dust and heat, listening to a Bible story, learning a scripture verse and repeating the Lord's Prayer.

Mabel also wrote each donor who sponsored a child at her school, no matter how small an amount was given. She solicited funds with her stories rather than asking for money, and habitually hand-wrote more than twenty letters a day. During some years Mabel accomplished the unthinkable marathon, raising enough money through her letters to keep a thousand boys in school per year. She also sent regular updates to the director of missionary outreach at home, R. E. Diffendorfer.

During these years she also carried on a lively correspondence with Mahatma Gandhi on education and disciplinary matters. To attribute to one individual Mabel's full-time profession as educator, administrator, innovator, fund-raiser and nurse to her boys in the boarding school stretches the imagination. Mabel Jones did it all with extraordinary dignity in primitive circumstances.

Mabel loved her books, frequently loaning them even to young British soldiers in the cantonment until they were ragged with use. Her dream of a library for her schoolboys prompted her to request children in Sunday schools in the U.S. to adopt the project and send books, resulting in a movement to establish libraries in schools throughout India.

Eunice recalls her own love of books. Mabel allowed a half hour of reading in bed for Eunice in her sleeping quarters on the rooftop before extinguishing her lamp. Mabel—being a mother—likely realized that moonlight provided surreptitious reading beyond the permitted time for several nights each month for her little girl.

About fifty miles north of the city of Lucknow, the town of Sitapur had three sections, including the bazaar with its shops, crowded with Indian families living in close contact with one another; the civil lines including exotic parks and gracious homes where the British lived and the mission was located; and a military cantonment about five miles out of the town. During World War I, Sitapur had one of the first flying fields in India where the English taught their young men to fly. Stanley and Eunice enjoyed watching the strange new machines ascend from the grass field.

Nearby, the Company Gardens with its lush produce and delightful fruit trees bordered the mission compound; both properties ended on the banks of the small Sarayan river. A grand grove of trees provided fruit such as mangoes and guavas, pomegranates and papayas that was sold with the vegetable produce to support the gardens.

Meanwhile, Eunice with her bouncy golden locks soon toddled her way into everyone's heart and attention. While Mabel poured herself into her boys at the school, about forty-five of whom were orphans, she carefully avoided lavishing praise on her little daughter, lest she become "spoiled." Being the strict teacher and disciplinarian that she was, at times Mabel administered "a little spanking"—of little consequence, as Eunice would run to her trusted Indian friends who subsequently scooped her up in their arms to comfort and caress her. Learning early that she could get anything and everything from them, Eunice says she never felt neglected, but grew in an atmosphere of love and affection, while still receiving appropriate discipline.

Eunice and her ayah spent the days exploring and playing on the compound. "Mother succeeded in not spoiling me," Eunice says, "but I was spoiled on the Indian side." This often worked itself out in the cookhouse that was separate from the big house. Although Mabel forbad Eunice to eat the spicy foods the Indians prepared, while Mabel was at the school the cook and others invited her to eat with them. They posted a guard outside, and when the memsahib hurried up the path from the school, they hurried Eunice away, her little tummy burning with the delights of the hot Indian dishes she loves to this day.

Her infractions concerning her mother's rules—now buried in nearly a century of passing years—now amuse her. "I think I was a perverse child; I did things that I knew my mother would not want me to do. I was simply unafraid."

Eunice's primary spoken languages were Hindustani and English. Bhulan the Muslim cook took seriously his role to teach Eunice to talk. Carrying her about the house, he pointed to various objects, stating their names in Urdu or Hindustani, enjoying her quick childish response and ready wit, each adoring the other.

Spoken primarily in north India, Hindustani is a spoken, but not formally written language. When it is written, words are spelled phonetically in English letters. ***Hindi*** derives its formal vocabulary from Sanskrit, while Urdu derivation is mostly Persian. In learning to read and write formally, Indian children are taught to write Hindi, which drops down from a bar and reads from left to right. Urdu is Arabic cursive, written from right to left above the line. In first grade all North Indian children learn Urdu and Hindi, with English added in the third grade. During colonial rule, most British children were sent back to England by the age of five or six for their formative education.

A cursory look at Sitapur and the school and grounds of the mission belies the hardships experienced in the early twentieth century. But the house itself increasingly frightened Mabel. Her daughter Eunice experienced too many close calls with those other inhabitants of the house: snakes.

Chapter 3

Of Snakes and Snafus

I will command my angels to guard you . . .
you'll tread on the young lion as easily as one does a cobra;
you'll trample down both lion and serpent.
—Yahweh

Sitapur was known as "snake city." Mabel had already experienced living with snakes before Eunice was born. One night the servants called her out to attend to a disagreement among them. She grabbed a robe in the dark—the one without its rope belt. Standing on the verandah talking, she felt something land on her long hair coiled on top of her head. Thinking it was a bird, for many built nests in the thatched roof, she pushed it gently off her head, but as it slithered down her bare back inside her robe rather than falling like a bird, she shook it through to the floor. In the excitement, the night caller's lantern was extinguished, leaving the two frantically attempting to avoid any rampage from the disturbed snake.

Once bitten, the victim dies within 28 minutes from the venomous bite of the twelve-inch, brown, slender ***karait***. The advantage of being bitten by a cobra was slight, with death following a bite by a cobra in 30 minutes. Had Mabel worn the belted robe, the karait likely would have done its fatal work, trapped around her mid-section by the belt.

Built with mud brick and whitewashed, the first mission house had once belonged to an Englishman who deeded it to the mission when he returned home. Not out of any altruistic motive, he simply preferred to donate it to a poor mission rather than let it fall into the hands of an Indian. Such was that relationship.

Hard, "clean" mud floors stretched throughout, but because both the mortar for the bricks and the floor itself were mud, scorpions and centipedes, insects and lizards felt welcome to live inside with the family. The stamped mud floors provided rats a playground for digging holes in which a variety of snakes set up housekeeping. With the assistance of the Muslim helpers—for no Hindu would kill a sacred cobra—Mabel killed more than forty serpents in and around the mission house.

One day Mabel told the Hindu sweeper that the sahib had seen a cobra in one of the holes in the mud brick walls. She planned to ask the Muslim helper to kill it, but knew the Hindu could find it.

So began the mother of all snake tours as he led Mabel throughout the mission house. He pointed to one of the holes in the mud brick.

"One lives here," he said. "That's all right. It won't hurt you."

Why is that?" Mabel asked.

Well, Memsahib, because I feed all of them every day."

You feed them?" Her voice quavered. "Show me some other holes where you feed the snakes."

So he took her to the office and removed a few books from the bookcase. There it was, a large, gaping hole holding a clay bowl—empty. "See, it has already eaten. I fill it with milk every day."

Feeling panic burn her throat like hot lava, she gently asked whether there were others. He took her next to her own bedroom closet. Moving a few towels to one side, he explained, "See, this bowl is empty, too. It's all right. They don't hurt you."

On and on, he led her to other feeding stations, although he must have realized her intent. Her resolve fired. She led a major project to fill all the holes and half-way up the walls with cement. But before she completed the work, one of the servants rolled over on a cobra in bed one night, was bitten and died.

After Mabel's baby arrived, snakes continued to appear, such as in the bathroom where the family threw used water into a brick-lined hole with an opening to the outside. Taking advantage of the cool, damp environment with an ideal entrance at ground level, they often wrapped themselves around the large Ali Baba earthenware jug used to store clean water.

In addition to her work at the school, Mabel busied herself during Eunice's early years with completing some of her projects that to her were necessary for the welfare of her schoolboys and her daughter. Having inherited some of her Canadian grandfather's practical ability as a builder, she planned and directed the building of a long-needed septic system as well as the Persian water wheel about which she had read.

Next, Mabel built another mission house, nearer the school. The opening on the floor of the bathroom, as well as all the doors were covered with fine mesh screens. She covered the mud brick walls and floor with cement and showed the workers how to make cement squares in black and white, or red and yellow rather than plain, cement-gray. Often called in the night to respond to a sick child or other problems, Mabel reasoned that a well-built house close to the boys' quarters solved two problems: too great a distance to her boys and the prevalence of snakes—or so she thought.

But even in the new house the snakes occasionally found them. Eunice still remembers nearly ninety years later climbing onto the sofa for a nap in her father's study. As the pillows were too high, she removed the top pillow, only to see a deadly karait coiled on the next pillow. When she told her mother that a snake was asleep on her pillow, Mabel really didn't believe her imaginative daughter, but checked anyway to assuage her daughter's fears. Thanks to that decision, we still have Eunice Jones Mathews today.

The mission house with its broad verandah that stretched across the width of the house imposed itself on the landscape. Tall doors marked entrances and small windows hugged the wall near the high ceiling. Identical houses were scattered in towns of all sizes in British India, all with one floor and a flat roof for cooler sleeping in the summer. The drawing room was the largest of the six rooms, while an office, a dining room and three bedrooms, each with private bath—sans running water—completed the suite.

Every room of the big house proved useful, including the imposing verandah. Both the tailor and the coolie reigned over it, each with a vital job. But both aged with the house and the time came to relieve the old blind man who controlled the "air conditioning" for the house. More and more often he fell asleep on the job in the hot summer steam, forgetting to pull the rope to move the punkah to fan the hot air.

Yet, Mabel could not turn him away, as he had served her as well as he could since she found him and his family begging in the marketplace. So, she offered to continue giving him his salary, while offering full retirement. He would hear none of it. "God gave me this work and I will do it until I die. I've worked for you all these years, Memsahib, and I would not leave you now," he told her as he gazed upward with opaque, unseeing eyes.

As he dozed off again, Mabel wrote in her newsletter, "Sometimes when he dozes and I suffocate with the hot air, and then when he suddenly arouses and pulls like a hurricane over my dripping body, I wonder who will die first."

The aging tailor also sat on the porch of the mission house, working for sixteen cents a day, patching and sewing clothes for the schoolboys. When the time came for him to leave her employ, Mabel entreated the women at home to help with just one of the three necessities: clothing. She raised much of the food with the boys' help, and she provided shelter for them, but they needed clothing—used or new.

Donations from home helped, but often dwindled or became no longer profitable when duty fees became exorbitant. So, Mabel taught the boys to make their own clothes, a task that sucked up more of her precious time than she wanted to expend on that mundane, though necessary work. As a result of daily "patching bees," her boys were "fearfully and wonderfully patched up. Sometimes, you have a hard time finding any of the original cloth on a garment!" Mabel wrote.

While tending the boys at the school along with her little daughter, Mabel agreed to community service as well. The Secretary of the Executive Board for Northern Asia recognized Mabel as counselor-at-large to Sitapur Methodism. She served as a member of the Red Cross Society, the Public Health Committee and the Baby Week Committee, on which she appeared—strangely enough—as the only woman, the only foreigner and certainly the only Christian. Then, she agreed to visit women in the jail and was appointed to the District Board with its oversight of the roads, schools, hospitals, dispensaries and other public facilities that served more than a million people.

One day Mabel lunched with His Excellency Sir Malcolm Hailey at the District Magistrate's home. As she chatted with friends, a Muslim official thanked Mabel for the book she had given him to read about the life of Christ. He said, "I have almost finished the book and I must say that I am sorry and disappointed that I can find nothing in it of which I disapprove."

Mabel learned that literature and music opened the door to conversation about Christ. Well-versed in both Urdu and Hindi, Mabel read the ***Bhagavad-Gita*** and knew the ***Qur'an*** quite well. "She knew full well," wrote Bishop James Mathews, "that one could not hope to witness effectively to what she knew was sacred for Christians without a deep comprehension of what Hindus regard as sacred. Too often this has escaped the missionary."

Meanwhile, little Eunice grew, her mischievous streak adding to her spunk. She early on rebelled against some of the protocol and discrimination and societal norms. Calling card had a distinct meaning in the early twentieth century. The servant from another household would deliver the calling card of a woman who desired to call on the recipient, who in return sent her card with the servant, naming a time for a visit, perhaps with lunch or tea.

On one occasion, a woman evangelist did more than "call" on Mabel. She moved in—much to Eunice's distress. Mabel and other missionaries had settled into small apartments in an old sanitarium in the cooler mountains during the hottest summer months for school vacation. On Saturday afternoons, one of the adults took Eunice and her friends to see black and white children's movies. Accompanied by alternately lively allegro and adagio piano music, the otherwise silent films captivated the children.

The visiting missionary woman expressed outrage at Eunice's favorite—and entirely too worldly—pastime, adding to Eunice's consternation with the bossy woman. "Movies are of the devil!" she preached at Mabel. "No matter who makes them, if it comes out of Hollywood, the children should not attend."

Rather than argue with her guest, Mabel relented. After the visiting evangelist had ruined several Saturdays for Eunice, her rage toward the woman bubbled up close to the boiling point. One day while Mabel and her friend attended a meeting together, a servant ran to Eunice exclaiming, "Oh ***baba***, I've just killed a snake!" Sure enough, it was a karait, very much dead, but still writhing.

"That's when the devil entered me," Eunice still remembers. Knowing that the dead snake could continue its autonomic movement for some time, Eunice retrieved it and lifted it onto the doorsill, closing the screen so it was not visible.

"No, no! You must not do this! You'll get in trouble," the helpers pleaded with her before vanishing as they saw Mabel and the woman walking toward the apartment door. Eunice hid nearby to watch her revenge in action.

The woman preceded Mabel, flung open the door and stepped on the snake. Fully cooperating, the dead karait wrapped its tail around her leg to the tune of unearthly, ghastly screams bursting from the visitor. Unfortunately for Eunice, she could not contain her laughter. Although her behavior merited a spanking, Eunice thought her prank was worth the trouble. Afternoon movies were resumed the following Saturday.

One day the gardener brought a tiny creature to Eunice that he had found when he mistakenly dug up his nest. Never having seen a mongoose so small, even Mabel agreed that it might be an inside-pet, the first, last and only—Mabel made that clear to all. Their lives spared, Eunice and her mother settled into a mutual acceptance of an unexpected family pet that would serve them well.

So, not only Eunice but also Mabel welcomed this mortal enemy of snakes into the household. Bhulan the cook helped with its food and care. Completely at home and named for Kipling's Rikki Tikki Tavi, the mongoose ran to Eunice and the helpers whenever they called his name. Since Rikki's natural habitat was any dark hole in the ground, he burrowed comfortably into any cozy corner, at night sleeping curled around Eunice's toes, a warm and soft comforter. Daytime found the devoted two-some together constantly, with Rikki curled around Eunice's neck most of the time.

The snakes disappeared magically. Everyone was happy, likely even the snakes who could finally live out a normal lifespan if they lived outdoors, thus avoiding Rikki. But once again, a visiting woman who feared everything in her strange new environment, became Eunice's nemesis. Mabel had neglected to warn the woman that all through the night the nearby orchard owners frightened away the flying bats that would eat the ripe guavas. The method was simple and loud enough to frighten any unsuspecting visitor. Filling tin cans with stones and attaching them to the trees with long ropes, through the night they yanked the ropes, triggering fright in both bats and unwary humans. Awakened with the racket, the screaming visitor thought a riot was occurring and that all were doomed to extermination.

During the excitement in the household, Rikki changed beds. When the exhausted and finally calm woman climbed back into bed and pushed her feet toward the bottom of the mattress, Rikki nipped at her foot. Assuming it was a fatal snakebite, the terrified woman was convinced that death stalked her. Discovering that it was "only Rikki" failed to reassure her.

So Rikki faced his Waterloo while Eunice comforted him and Mother Mabel made plans. Unfortunately for Rikki, several others shared history of having been nipped on the feet, as everyone went barefooted in the house. Enough was enough. Rikki had to go. After numerous attempts to give Rikki away, he always found his way back home and into the arms of his true love. As he sat waiting at the door to be admitted back into the family circus, the servants returned him to the ecstatic Eunice. Of course Mabel always discovered his return and repeatedly tried to re-locate Rikki. Finally during school vacation, schoolboys carried him to their village, much too great a distance for Rikki to find his way back into Eunice's waiting arms and aching heart. However, it must be noted that Eunice's tears were exceeded only by her mother's at the loss of their useful pet.

Eunice's need for a pet prompted another experiment—an "outside" monkey that preferred an inside playground. When outdoors, he jumped like a tightly wound spring into a tree and then swung down onto Eunice, knocking her to the ground—very hard on dresses and knees. Eunice thought she understood his chatter as he jumped from her shoulders to chase an imagined creature with his mistress in tow.

When he managed to escape into the house, he leapt to the curtains and swung with glee. Finding the piano, he went wild with delight, jabbering and racing from end to end on the keyboard. To this day joy fills those memories, except that—alas—he too was sent miles away on a train, while Eunice looked in vain for his return.

In one letter describing a typical day, Mabel wrote about the monkeys—and the attitudes of both Muslim and Hindu workers: "Shrieking and yelling and imploring in the garden: 'Monkeys!' the Hindu gardener yells. 'Oh my nephews! Go! Go! Please leave us!' [while] the Muslim watchman shrieks like a demon and throws broken bricks. Monkeys are hardly sacred to him."

One day while shopping at a village bazaar with her mother for school supplies, Eunice glimpsed a pair of rabbits with soft, white fur and red eyes pleading to go home with her. When Mabel questioned the salesman about their gender, he promised solemnly, "They are brothers, I swear by the beard of ***Allah***." This was the ultimate pledge.

One morning Eunice ran to her mother to announce that someone had put ten tiny other creatures in the rabbit pen. Mabel was not pleased with what she saw. She enlarged the cage and was satisfied until the now one dozen bunnies began digging under the cage—and in their spare time birthed more babies. Frantic when they discovered the garden where she raised food for the boys, Mabel began giving them to the students to take to their villages. Years later while visiting India during college years, Eunice met many old friends who said their villages still had white rabbits from those two "brothers."

Eunice's pair of peacocks roamed about the outdoors. But on the roof where she slept in a small room with her birdcage, she never knew when, in the wee hours of the morning, her birds would start their singing—or talking—the myna bird waking her with "hello" followed quickly by "good-bye."

Birds on the roof—not so bad. But then, knowing her love for animals, someone gave a tiny deer to Eunice. Again Mabel cringed, for the deer decided Eunice was to be its mother. When Eunice went indoors, the pet deer curled up on the verandah until she reappeared. It danced about with joy and rubbed its head on Eunice. Unfortunately, it drank too much water one hot day and did not survive. When someone offered a replacement, without consulting her daughter Mabel gave a resounding "No!"

* * * * *

While she had no fear of animals, Eunice cowered from two intense fears that followed her even into college years. One day when Eunice was about two years old on their return trip from the family's first furlough in the States, they stopped in Japan. A wooden Shintu temple suddenly went up in flames. Thinking the sight would intrigue the little girl, Stanley rushed with her to the site of the raging gargantuan fire. Terrified, for years she battled nightmares and a fear of wooden structures.

Her second fear was rooted in the terrifying image of the goddess ***Kali***, the goddess of destruction. Blood poured from her mouth and she rested one foot on creatures she had beheaded. Eunice's ayah was a Hindu, and she often threatened Eunice, "If you don't do what I tell you, I will see that Kali gets you." Kali's image was visible everywhere in local Hindu shops and terrified the young child on every shopping day.

What was it about this little girl who adored her animal friends, but rejected the fire and smoke and places where the wild things are? Might this trait have been a prescient lens on the larger world in which she would grow up to become a lover of all God's creatures and all peoples, and who would learn to commit those "wild things" to God who likewise abhors pain, suffering, fear, tragedy?

Because tragedies do come, unbidden, unwelcome, unexpected, as Mabel and Eunice in Sitapur were about to experience.

Chapter 4

Catching Fish and Cooking Grain

When all around my soul gives 'way,
God then is all my hope and stay . . .
—Edward Mote

Sometimes seasons do not meet expectations. When the monsoons refuse to arrive, the Indian people struggle through drought and famine. At other times, as the people pray to their gods for rain, a flood surprises them. Such was the night in late summer 1923.

Bishop Jaswant Chitambar, E. Stanley Jones and Bishop Waskom Pickett met in Arrah for a meeting and stayed to pray with concerned people for much needed rain. About 4:30 in the morning as they slept on the roof of the mission house, Pickett awoke to the sound of water running. It had not rained. The river Ganges was eight miles away and the Sone River ten miles distant emptied into the Ganges.

The others soon awoke, and checking further, they saw a mystery river not forty feet from the mission house. Rising seven inches per hour, it demanded quick action. They began moving the boarding school students to the mission house, then onto the roof, where the boys spent the next three days and nights. While some women had been rescued about midnight of the first day of the flood, soon nearly a hundred more had taken refuge on the second story.

Cobras and other snakes washed into the house and—much to the dismay of Hindu friends—had to be killed. Drinking water was reclaimed by filling a bathtub with the contaminated water and, by adding alum, the filth settled to the bottom. They could then boil the water for tea or coffee. Pickett worked tirelessly, one day spending fifteen hours in the water, having made a raft to rescue some and to salvage bags of rice and wheat.

In an area more than 150 square miles around the mission in Arrah, more than 65 percent of the ***kacha*** houses collapsed. The mysterious river that appeared on that sunny, cloudless day was traced to a cloudburst more than 400 miles away.

Mabel was experiencing her own troubles while Stanley was in Arrah. A little creek named Sarayan, a quarter of a mile from the bungalow, was one of many tributaries of the Gumti River. The creek began to rise and before long, it filled the school house. The school boys climbed onto the roof while Mabel and Eunice took refuge in Missionary Hanson's house. Spared any loss of life or serious damage, the children and adults worked together to accomplish clean-up activity.

Before long, however, the waters again overflowed. After seven weeks of massive clean-up and salvaging as much as possible any school supplies, the waters dried up and the children moved in again. But a cloudburst followed. Mabel and Eunice with others took refuge on the roof, not realizing that water was fast filling the main floor. A friend with a house on higher ground demanded Mabel and Eunice move to her house, as the water was still rising. Grabbing a few clothes, they did so. The next morning they gasped to see their mission bungalow partially submerged.

This time Missionary Hanson and others with a squad of police pushed neck-deep through the snake-infested waters to rescue teachers and schoolboys. When the old dormitories collapsed, that disaster eventually moved them toward better living conditions for the boys.

Miraculously, again no lives were lost. As Mabel later wrote, "the widow's cruse did not fail," taken from the Old Testament story of the widow's oil that simply would not be diminished. Stories of other miracles followed. A pregnant woman had climbed a tree to escape the floods and managed—God only knows how—to deliver her own baby in the tree house.

Eunice still remembers one horrible mess when they returned to the house a week later. The furniture was piled against one wall, and unfortunately that was the wall with the door to the outside. When Mabel had built the new mission house, she made the doorsills several inches high to help block the entrance of small animals. Although the water had receded, an adequate depth provided a lovely pool for the fish.

Unadulterated delight filled eight year-old Eunice. Her menagerie now sported a living room full of fish cavorting about the premises. Climbing onto saturated chairs, she went fishing with her hands, gleefully scooping them up. While this amused and occupied Eunice, her mother was far less enamored with the situation. Mabel would have preferred destruction by fire, because one could begin again without attempting to salvage the saturated goods.

But Mabel's trials were just beginning. Although all of her boys had been rescued during the disaster, Mabel next discovered that her year's supply of the boys' staple food was totally submerged for days in the brick storeroom. She typically bought grain annually when at its lowest price and filled the storage room about three-quarters full. They would then scoop the grain through a small window as needed.

As the grain swelled in the steamy moist quarters, it also

cooked, pushing the walls outward, forcing the building off its foundation. Just short of collapsing entirely, the bulging walls survived when the moisture lessened. "I must see it for myself," Mabel insisted. The storehouse was indeed steaming, undoubtedly the world's largest rice cooker. But, what to do with all that cooked grain—that was the problem. Her boys and the mission personnel could not possibly eat a year's worth of grain before it spoiled. "Oh God, what shall I do?" she prayed earnestly.

As a result of the flood, whole villages had been devastated and untold numbers had drowned. As survivors crawled back to their villages, the news spread. "Tell the people I have food for them!" Mabel announced from the mission.

Before long, in the way of communicating that works better than modern cell phone, internet and telephone contact, the word spread. Long lines quickly formed at Mabel's door. Surviving villagers who had no food and no way to get any trekked to the mission. They came by the hundreds, some with vessels, and others with only the end of a ***sari*** or a loin cloth stretched out to the workers who poured out shovelfuls of cooked grain for the favored villagers who had survived the flood.

In any extremity, the nay-sayers prefer argument to action. "The grain will ferment," some had told Mabel. "You can never distribute that much!" others advised her. "Just throw it away!" they urged. But Mabel knew this was the answer to her prayer. She had lost her grain but would feed hundreds of starving villagers. And she thanked God.

In addition to her faith in God, her intellect, abilities and generous elbow grease, Mabel was gifted with prescience in certain events. One day when Eunice and two little friends went off to play, they did not return at the expected time. Somewhat frantic, the mothers of the three girls began to search, calling and reasoning that they couldn't have gone far. Even the little creek was hardly more than a trickle—when not flooded—for the girls could wade across it without difficulty.

As the mothers searched, Mabel pictured the children in what looked like a cave. She asked the mission watchman to take a ladder to a spot that she envisioned. Sure enough, when he arrived at the location, he leaned the ladder against the rocks and called to the children who answered him. They had wandered up the embankment and crept under the overhanging rock, and didn't know how to get down. Eunice recalls her fears and prayers to be found. Even Mabel's prescience counted as a God-given gift that led to the children.

Another instance in which Mabel's gift proved useful occurred in a day when communication, while a long shot from smoke signals, still depended on weeks-long journeys by ship to reach from one side of the world to another. One night Mabel dreamed of her grandfather whose relationship she treasured. Devastated when his granddaughter Mabel decided to go to India, he must have become increasingly saddened when her stay became a lifetime choice rather than a passing notion.

During Mabel's first year in the mission field, long before she and Stanley had met and married, she had shared a room with someone who heard Mabel call out suddenly in the night, "I'm coming! I'm coming, Grandfather!" Mabel had heard him calling her. "I did something stupid, and I slipped and fell . . ." he cried out.

Severely shaken, she marked the calendar with the time of her dream, prayed continually for him and the family at home and waited a full month before the letter arrived. With shaking hands she slit the envelope open and read the date on the letter, written on the day of her dream: "Grandfather went up to Devil's Hollow," his sister had written. Mabel knew the area, and did not approve of his going there alone, as it was dangerous walking and not within calling distance of the family. He had fallen and had called Mabel to help him. He told his rescuers, "I lay here and called for Mabel."

Once more the miracle of the human psyche testified to the Creator's involvement in the lives of God's children.

In addition to personal loss and stress, Mabel wrote home about the schoolboys. She felt privileged in comparison with the workers on the compound and families of most of the children who attended the mission school. She also found that a healthy sense of humor lubricates stressful events. In one letter she wrote,

"The boys on the right of me, all Hindus and Mohammedans [Muslims], are playing hockey, and the shouts of joy and pell-mell rushes show me that they are enjoying themselves as much as boys in any land. Eighty boys on the left of me are making noise enough over cricket and football to make a certain missionary . . . wonder whether she would not prefer a school of girls. The little boys behind me are trying to get a kite out of a clump of tall bamboos. And," she continued, "the little boys in front of me—alas! alas!—have been listening to a lecture on: Why didn't you get your geography lesson?"

But on other days, her distress was not alleviated with nonchalance and humor. Mabel related to someone that a high school boy dropped in for a chat. "News has come," he said, "that my wife, who still lives with her parents some distance from here, is ill, and I must go to her." Mabel discovered as she questioned him that he did not like being married to his little wife. She was only seven years old.

Another time a five year-old orphan boy was not thriving at the boarding school. Mabel placed little Birket in the home of one of the missionary women for some TLC and monitoring. The woman gave him a picture book that he treasured. One day she noticed his tears and asked him about his trouble. Sobbing, Birket explained he had given his precious book to the tailor to take to his sick son. Comforting him, she told him to get his cup so she could fill it with milk. When he returned he found another book on his mat and hugged it to himself. Kindness transforms.

Mabel wrote, too, of the boys who had discovered matches—oh, the joy and power of setting a fire to burning. However, as they could not find anything "appropriate" to burn, they set fire to their shirts.

Of course, they had to learn their lesson. Their playtime was curtailed for days while they pulled weeds until the gardener said,

"Enough. You pulled eight ***annas*** worth. Now you can ask for your shirts." The boys solemnly promised, "We'll never do it again." And they never did.

Discipline in the schools during the 19th and early 20th centuries included measures that today would be frowned upon, if not punishable by law in the United States. But finally after many requests and much cajoling, Mabel relented and listed in one of her newsletters some of the disciplinary measures she used. They included washing out the mouth with soap after a student used "dirty" words; using explanations, reasoning and praying; making the boys work to repay what they stole and ate; depriving them of little pleasures and sending them to bed.

Mabel, however, did not ordinarily employ corporal punishment, and wrote that "no teacher or matron or boy is allowed to strike with even a lead pencil." But on occasion both boys and teachers agree that "nothing will drive the spirit of Satan out as effectively as a hairbrush in the hands of the superintendent . . . sometimes the only thing that will save the child, dislike it as we may."

Eunice remembers very few "little spankings" by her mother, and suggests she is now sure each was well deserved and appropriately administered.

Much of Mabel's time—too much, she thought—involved gathering supplies for the school. At one point they had one box of twenty pencils that had to be shared among the groups. Providing adequate nourishment for her boys and for Eunice likewise occupied her thinking and planning. She divided chores among the boarding school students who weekly rotated jobs such as gardening and gathering food for the cook. In addition to fresh fruits and vegetables they grew or she could purchase from the market, Mabel served the students stewed lentils with oatmeal in the morning. For dinner, curried rice with onions was a staple.

Even the merchants respected Mabel in her endeavors, though they tried tempting her to unscrupulous actions. Her ingenuity and honesty earned her a reputation for getting what she wanted while never stooping to dishonest tactics. More than once she discovered a hundred rupee note in the bottom of the basket with the fruit she had ordered. She returned the basket with a note and the money that had been "mistakenly" placed in her basket, thanking them for the good fruit that her boys enjoyed. She would not acknowledge their attempts to entrap her, rather choosing to treat them with respect—deserved or not.

Another time Mabel was dismayed to find that many of the books in the school had become so old and tattered that she could no longer find enough fabric to stitch the leaves together again—no duct tape or Scotch tape there. The preachers, too, suffered hardship that she and Stanley attempted to ameliorate, but not always with success. Because of economic adversity, of more than one hundred pastors in one area, the numbers dwindled to seventeen. "I feel like crying," Mabel wrote. "Preachers for sale for $50/year! Boys for $30 . . ." But what a winning investment for the investor!

Not only did the ranks of local preachers dwindle, but also the decline of good schools distressed Mabel. She had depended on strong secondary schools as the next step in her boys' education. But with missionary ranks thinning, some schools had passed into the hands of Indians, some of whom executed their jobs splendidly, while others were unprepared for the rigors. In some instances, the schools had deteriorated into places not compatible with the Christian faith. Mabel did her best "to encourage or reprimand her students, to keep before them the highest ideals; to see that they are in the right environment, to get them into schools where they will get the best training; and to raise money to keep them there."

At times Mabel raised money by selling lumber to local builders. Her measures of frugality amused some, such as trimming the size of a student's envelope addressed to a donor so it could be sent for the equivalent of 2½ cents in U.S. coins rather than a pittance more. She likewise carefully disbursed funds, at one time offering fifteen annas for every snake killed—those creatures that would continue to be her nemesis.

Working within the caste system so firmly entrenched in the

culture, but so repugnant to Mabel's sensibilities, tried her patience and ingenuity. She did not always win. One day three coolies resigned because she had sent a schoolboy into the garden to pull weeds. From the sweeper caste, the child had been her student for five years. The three Hindu coolies had jobs that were vital to the compound: one to drive the oxen; one to lower the great pigskin bag into the well and empty it; and one to guide the water into areas in the garden needing water. Mabel could not dissuade them and had to accept their resignation. But in order to hire new coolies to save the garden, she eventually had to dismiss the student as well.

When Mabel knew the time had come for the nationals to assume responsibility for the mission school, she tried to relinquish her position. She would contribute in other ways. But the women teachers adamantly refused her plan. First of all, they argued, they would all resign if an Indian woman assumed the duties, so much did they respect Mabel Jones. Besides, "an Indian woman would be domineering," they explained, "and would not be permitted to teach or be in charge of the boys," reverting to earlier stigmas attached to women teachers and administrators that Mabel thought she had fought successfully. Yet these women teachers felt they owed their loyalty, as well as their positions to Mabel. Furthermore, the women teachers said an Indian woman would not have the stamina to work as hard as Mabel did, nor could she successfully correspond with donors and patrons to raise money from the United States.

So, that was that. Mabel was destined at that time and place to continue her selfless work in the Sitapur Mission. While Stanley had been appointed as the district superintendent of the Sitapur District, his difficult travels allowed him little time with the family. He also had returned to the states, away for eighteen months, preaching and soliciting funds for the work in India.

Eunice once wrote Miss Nellie Logan asking, "Have you seen much of my daddy since he has been in America? I haven't seen him for almost a whole year . . ." Miss Nellie was a family friend who had taught Stanley in his first year of school and become a loyal confidante and counselor. Stanley had once written of her: "Blessed is the person who can say, 'I have a friend.' I am very blessed, for I have a friend, a real friend, a lifelong friend, and the memory of her lingers like a benediction."

Meanwhile, Mabel wrote her own letter to the director of the Board of Missions: "I have just been reading the life of Bishop Taylor. If Mrs. Taylor could do without him for four years, I suppose we can [tolerate] eighteen months of separation for the sake of America," that was assumed needed him more than his family or the work in India. "But," Mabel pleaded, "please don't extend the time!" She could not have imagined that this was only a foretaste of what would come.

Even without father and husband, Eunice and Mabel managed not only acceptance, but also the challenge of surpassing even their own expectations. As the outdoor temperature rose to 110 degrees Fahrenheit in the shade, Mabel herself was suffering with quinsy—a severe inflammation of the throat and larynx that causes dyspnea and fever.

Then the cable arrived. They felt its force slamming them against a concrete wall that left them breathless and hurting. Mabel's husband and Eunice's father, a graduate of Asbury College in Wilmore, Kentucky, in the United States, had been elected a bishop at the General Conference of the Methodist Episcopal Church in 1928.

Young Eunice promptly wrote fourteen reasons why her father should not be a bishop. Mabel said, "All I could do was to pull the sheet over my head and indulge in a very feminine cry! But after a bit [there] came a feeling of peace that somehow things would turn out all right . . ."

So Mabel and Eunice prayed, believing still that God was in control. They believed St. Paul's affirmation: "All things work together for good to them that love God . . ." To their utter delight, the next cable arrived with this news: "Bishop" E. Stanley Jones on the following morning after a sleepless night had resigned, prior to consecration as bishop. Indeed, God had other plans for Stanley—and his family.

> As Mabel was the only one in Sitapur who could play the organ, she was pressed into service at the local English-speaking church. Eunice remembers well her own contribution to the service of Christian worship where she sat on the floor behind the organ, vigorously pumping the stiff pedals up and down. One never knows who's behind the bellows.
>
> The Church of England priest made monthly rounds to the little church, located near the military cantonment. Few children appeared, as the parents sent them back to England at an early age, lest they adopt an Indian-English accent. That always identified one as country-born or Anglo-Indian, both of which were considered beneath British dignity.
>
> Of course, each Sunday mother and daughter also attended the mission church located on the compound between the boys' school and the girls' school. The children, whose attendance was mandatory, marched to church in long lines.

Crises of every imaginable ilk threatened the health and survival of not only the Jones family, but also of their mission in a troubled world. Yet Mabel's faith fortified her for all manner of adversity. She had written of the flood, "I feel absolutely dismayed at our terrible loss. But God has provided in the past and He surely will again." Mabel later wrote, "God has always supplied all our needs, and we can trust Him for the future. If I should ever have any doubts about the efficiency of prayer and faith, they would at once vanish at the memory of the way our needs have been met . . . No child has ever gone hungry in our school, and we have no bills. It gives us confidence for the future and keeps us from worrying."

Mabel's faith would continue to be tested like gold in the fire. She once wrote: "There have been times when I felt that physically, I could not carry on. And then there would come an influx of strength that would carry me through the day, and I knew someone had been praying. There have been times when it seemed that money was an absolute necessity for His work's sake, and the box was empty. Not only that, but there were bills unpaid and obligations that could not be met. And then the home mail would come with a check and I knew that He had put the burden on someone's heart even before I prayed! What a reservoir of power there is in earnest prayer!"

While not believing that prayer is merely a last resort to be employed only when other methods fail, Mabel was nonetheless surprised by some miraculous answers. One day when she was in desperate need, a letter arrived that described a dream in which the writer had seen Mabel, looking greatly troubled. When the woman awoke, she sent two hundred dollars, recognizing the dream as a divine message.

* * * * *

While Eunice transformed the Great Flood into the sport of fishing in her living room, it would take more than a child's imagination to sustain Mabel's faith in the coming storm. In addition to personal needs, poverty, disease, politics and natural disasters, the whole world seemed intent on going to war—World War I. India was pregnant with the great revolution fathered by Mohandas Karamchand Gandhi that would change the face of the country. Then another cataclysmic event hit their world.

The Jones family never imagined that the worst was yet to come.

Chapter 5

Rampaging Cataclysms

Though I walk through the valley of the shadow of death
I will fear no evil, for thou art with me.
—King David

They never saw it coming. For one thing, Mabel was accustomed to being called on in the middle of the night to tend to a sick child. Having adapted to acting nurse and even doctor, Mabel knew how to treat typical ailments of elementary school children. In fact, as news of her medical prowess reached the villages through her students, she also became the on-call "doctor" for an extended community. Although she disliked "anything to do with medicine or disease, when folks walk miles for help and are likely to die without it, what can one do?" she asked.

For starters, she read and studied, spending vacation time with a doctor friend who loaned medical books to Mabel to increase her knowledge. Whenever she referred a patient with a note to the government hospital about ten miles distant that had one surgeon, they saw the person immediately, trusting Mabel's judgment. One man walked nine miles from his village to request medicine for his wife with a fever. She gave medicine for malaria, but after a second nine-mile trek, he informed her that his wife had smallpox, too. He had not mentioned it earlier, because he only wanted something for her fever.

Snakebite, too, was common, reported to have killed more than forty-seven thousand in India in the year 1929, but no children were bitten in Mabel's more than twenty years at the school. One morning the shed skin of the dreaded karait snake was found clinging to an account book that Mabel customarily pulled from a cabinet without looking. While such incidents sometimes left her breathless, Mabel thanked God for each escape.

To address the medical needs, Mabel spent hours "mixing magnesium sulphate and vaseline for boils, sulphur and Vaseline for itch, quinine and water with sulphuric acid for malaria, weighing out protargol lotion for inflamed eyes, measuring out bismuth and sall for dysentery, pouring out castor oil and counting out cascara pills."

But one day she was called to attend to a schoolboy, writhing in abdominal pain and vomiting that could leave a child vulnerable to dehydration with serious results. That she knew. She treated the child with the usual remedies for dysenteric attack, for which there could be many causes, isolated him from the others and forced fluids. But within hours, the boy was dead.

Devastated, Mabel nearly panicked on hearing the news of cholera's rampage, by then traveling at the speed of light, settling over the mission, the nation and the world like a pall of death. Within six weeks, the Sitapur District lost ten thousand to cholera.

The Indians' "only remedy was to beat tom-toms and worship frantically before the goddess of cholera, that her anger might be turned away . . ." When a doctor arrived to help intervene, Mabel reported, he started an intravenous saline solution into one boy already blue with the pallor of death; fortunately, that child revived and eventually recovered. In addition to palliative treatment, the time would come when inoculations became available against many of the diseases that wiped out thousands without regard for status or caste, race or religion.

In desperation Mabel began sending telegrams to the parents of the well children to inform them of the situation and to expect their children's arrival to protect them and also prevent the disease from spreading. But one child after another died on reaching home, having already been exposed. Mabel watched James Sunder Lall run happily to his train and home where he would be spared. Mabel rejoiced at the escape of any. She learned that the boy reached home safely, but news soon arrived that he "died at midnight . . . Noble Briscoe and Solomon Har Daal, splendid sons of our preachers, and dear little Dar Chote Lall left in seemingly the best of health, but [were] dead the next day."

"Each day brought more cases and more deaths until I felt I could bear no more," she wrote. "My splendid boys, bright, clean, healthy, happy, promising little lads who had been with me until they seemed like my own sons, [were] snatched away while we stood helpless. I had nursed the boys through forty-two cases of influenza, thirty-six with small pox, [plus] measles, mumps, malaria and all sorts of complaints, and we had saved them all, but this"—she wrote—"this was far more terrible . . ."

Mabel also carried the burden of triage, deciding which child would live, as they could only treat one child at a time. They lost more than forty children in the school. The teachers, themselves hardly more than young girls, worked alongside Mabel day and night with little thought of their own danger. Diet—for those who could eat—consisted of cooked potatoes and onions, avoiding greens and other fresh foods that could harbor cholera.

When thoughts of the possibility of losing her own young daughter crashed over Mabel in life-threatening waves, she felt the futility of her remedies that seemed no better than scattered sandbags to stem the flood of cholera. In spite of prayers and work to save a few, she trembled as she watched the disease break through every defense against the catastrophic tragedy that washed over India.

The etiology of the plague that killed one third of Europe's population was not immediately suspected to be related to contaminated water, food, poor sanitation, rats, garbage and human waste. But Hippocrates about 350 B.C.E. first noted that boiling water helps avoid certain diseases, although he did not identify the reason. Centuries later, the connection between disease and microorganisms was noted by physician John Snow who traced cholera to contaminated water. Finally in 1876 a German doctor, Robert Koch, identified the comma-shaped bacillus under microscopic examination.

It was not the first time in history that Death stalked the earth in the guise of cholera. Not the same but as devastating as other pandemics in the 6th, 16th and 17th centuries, cholera this time had begun its march across India in 1917 in ***Calcutta,*** where pilgrims had gathered for the ***Kumbh festival***. Sharing close living quarters, contaminated water and poor sanitation, many Indians experienced abdominal pain that often progressed to death within hours. Survivors then carried the disease back to their villages, and so it spread. Hundreds of thousands of Indians perished, in addition to more than ten thousand British troops stationed in India.

The Industrial Revolution with its improved transportation also paved a smoother road to a global pandemic. The world was shrinking. The disease traveled into Russia and throughout Europe, triggering a fear once more of this dreaded disease of earlier centuries. In Paris one wrote of the "public halls filled with dead bodies . . . with long lines of hearses in queue." Spread to the United States by way of infected ships, one man wrote in New York City that he pitched forward in the street "as if knocked down with an axe. I had no premonition at all," he said.

Eunice herself survived a variety of tropical and other ailments such as sprue, smallpox, dysentery, malaria and typhoid, before coming down with what Dr. Butcher—that same doctor who delivered Eunice in 1914—diagnosed as tuberculosis. But Eunice doubts to this day that her bouts with respiratory distress were attributable to TB. She did escape some typical Western children's diseases, such as measles and mumps, although some of the Indian boys succumbed to such diseases. Over time, Eunice obviously built up a strong immune system bolstered by her mother's watchful eye and plentiful doses of cod liver oil, liver extract and "every other evil-smelling and evil-tasting brews," Eunice still remembers.

Not only did cholera attack, but also the great influenza epidemic ravaged the United States populace, killing more than 675,000 in 1919. But few know that of the 22 million who died worldwide from this especially virulent strain, more than half were in India.

The combination of cholera and influenza presented a new challenge, for soon scores of children were left without parents. Hospitals and missions nearly drowned in the flood of babies who demanded care, lest they die in the streets of starvation and disease. Two Indian Methodist Conferences quickly raised funds for the "Warne Baby Fold," named for Bishop Frank Warne. Still in operation today, the home lists an impressive roster of children who as adults have served the church well.

Further complicating the problems of disease and loss of life, donations for these missions had dwindled to a trickle as world events clogged the flow of funds during the World Wars. During these black days affecting Europe and the United States in the early twentieth century, World War I, known as the Great War, shaped the lives of Indians as well as the British and missionaries living in the subcontinent. Arthur McPhee wrote of the war's "negative impact on missions, on family life, fund-raising, costs, communications, workloads, international travel, replacement personnel, and even politics. Inflation grew with the termination of the German market for exports. Great Britain . . . required huge amounts of wheat and other crops to feed its troops, thereby causing a food shortage, even famine among Indians. Profiteering, speculating, and hoarding" increased; medicines were unavailable; taxes escalated.

Then the stock market crash in 1929 and the Great Depression in the United States hit like a tsunami, wiping out even the meager donations that had kept the mission school afloat. Knowing that support for her five hundred boys had dropped precipitously while she was in the States on her first furlough, Mabel had no choice but to continue translating the boys' simple thank-you letters from Hindustani into English, and to answer hundreds of others to maintain the work. Increasingly, prayer for the missionaries became easier than financial support, yet both were vital to survival.

Questioned by the New York office about overlooking a stack of field mail from the mission board during these trying days, Mabel explained, "I suspect that few missionaries [have] as much desk work as I have, a boarding school with more than a hundred boys, eight to fifteen medical cases a day, all my husband's mail to attend to (he is never home), a house to look after, a little girl to educate, a farm to run and a dozen interviews a day—I do not get much time for reading!"

Also during those years, Stanley suffered a ruptured appendix, complicated by tetanus (lockjaw) that can be fatal. Then headaches began to plague him, and mental lapses while preaching forced him to sit down until his memory cleared. Added to this, he was named an agent of the Methodist Publishing House in Lucknow and was given the additional task of providing salaries of five hundred workers in the districts he superintended. He also began to feel the pressure of an expanded call to minister to the intelligentsia of India following a conversation in which a Hindu judge asked him, "Why don't you come to us?" Stanley had not realized they wanted his message, so he had "taken the line of least resistance—the outcastes." The judge replied that Stanley was mistaken. " . . . we do want you . . . provided you come in the right way"—without bias or arrogance. And so he did, winning their respect.

While considering this outreach as a mandate, Stanley weighed what it meant in light of his already demanding work and travels throughout the districts he superintended. He wrote that he finally collapsed due to a "spiritual sag" that led to a "physical sag." He further wrote that "a sense of hopelessness has crept over the soul of India," and he believed that from thence it seeped into his own spirit. Or, being only human, might the converse have been true? Stanley had endured mounting physical maladies and a crushing workload that resulted in spiritual "dis-ease" [sic].

Although Stanley had passed examinations in Urdu and Hindi, the languages had not yet become a part of him. "I preached what I could say, not what I wanted to say," he lamented. Following several attempts at rest in the mountains, he finally took furlough time. "I ended up after eight years with a call and a collapse," he wrote, and—we might add—a wife and a daughter. Assuming he was renewed after a respite in the States, Stanley returned to India, but headaches and fatigue returned with a vengeance.

Stanley credited his healing, fortunate for all, to the Indian evangelist Rev. Tamil David whose message pierced his weary heart. "The secret to avoiding physical and mental fatigue," David had said, was "to relax, keep free from tension, and draw on inner spiritual reserves."

Inner spiritual reserves? Stanley questioned whether he possessed that capital, and he believed he heard God's voice questioning him:

"Are you ready for the work to which God has called you?"

"No," Stanley answered honestly. "I'm done for. I've reached the end of my resources and I can't go on."

"If you'll turn that problem over to me and not worry about it, I'll take care of it."

"Lord, I close the bargain right now."

A sense of peace and power flooded his being as he arose from his knees a well man.

David Bundy discerned another side to Stanley's survival. Convinced of Mabel's extraordinary importance to Stanley's ministry, he stated that except for her, Stanley probably would have been sent home as a "missionary failure." The dark night of the soul nearly felled him, but it did not. As a result of God's grace and Mabel's tenacity, E. Stanley Jones endured to bless the world with his prolific writing and relevant preaching.

Strong as she was, and thankful for Stanley's recovery, Mabel ably nursed her boys through catastrophic illnesses and young Eunice through typhoid fever. Somehow in God's mercy she and Eunice escaped the cholera and influenza that attacked her boys, the continent and beyond. However at one point, aches and pains injected Mabel's every movement as the result of a fall while carrying a heavy lantern on her way to tend to one of the boys. She had slipped on wet bricks, and for weeks nursed broken ribs and a dented ear bone. Fortunately, before she lost consciousness she flung herself away from the flames that ignited within inches of her head.

As Mabel swung precariously over the precipice of pain for herself and the valley of the shadow of death for those she loved, her rope finally frayed and she plunged toward disaster. Caught mercifully by a God-send, Mabel and Eunice on doctor's strict orders left the mission to the Rockeys, a missionary couple, and retired to recover in Landour in the ***Himalayas***. There the cool air and sunshine proved to be the respite they needed.

"I plan on going down the first of September," Mabel wrote from there, "to gather the scattered remains of my flock and begin again . . . Mr. Jones [the formal manner of referring to one's spouse for that cohort], "has returned to his evangelistic work and does not expect to be home until the middle of October."

The physical and emotional strain on both Mabel and Stanley might have ended their ministry, but they continued to practice St. Paul's declaration: "I can do all things . . ." an arrogant assertion were it not for the nucleus of his quote: " . . . through Christ who strengthens me."

* * * * *

Something else was happening in India. The whole world recognized Mohandas K. Gandhi, who became known by endearing names such as Mahatma (Great Soul) and ***Gandhiji*** (Beloved). Few picture him as a well-educated, finely dressed lawyer, trained in England, working in South Africa. Rather, they see him as the wizened, bony man clad in a loincloth, walking the dusty roads of India with staff in hand.

Salman Rushdie described this image when he wrote that Gandhi was a "passionate opponent of modernity and technology, preferring the pencil to the typewriter, the loincloth to the business suit, the plowed field to the belching manufactory."

Many envision the spinning wheel, the ***charkha***, that symbolized Gandhi's ***Quit India*** campaign that would eventually dramatically change his country. Because the Indians had become inextricably trapped into economic and political dependence on Britain, Gandhi thoughtfully devised a way out, a way for millions to refuse domination by the British—yet without violence. ***Swaraj*** (home rule), Gandhi wrote, "is unattainable without the beautiful art [of spinning] becoming universal in India."

Without digging deeper one wonders at the sense of his logic. The national Congress flag, designed primarily by Gandhi, symbolizes unity, non-violence and identification through the charkha (spinning wheel) with the highest and lowliest in the land: the green representing Indian Muslims; the saffron stripe the Hindus; and the middle white stripe for all others. Central though, is the image of the spinning wheel, and the banner itself, of homespun, ***khadi***.

"Spinning was the sun of his solar system," said Tendulkar. The poor could spin (even with a hand-held spinner); the rich could spin. The result of spinning produced "homespun," symbolizing "unity [for all] . . . prosperity [regardless of caste] . . . non-violence [the only right approach] . . . body-labour [sic] [the means of sustenance] . . . simplicity [to strengthen both body and soul]. . . human dignity and economic freedom [to sever the bonds of servitude] . . ." even acting as a "substitute for gun powder."

Spinning, he believed, could even free women from sex trade and beggars from the streets.

Deemed a sacrament—a social, moral, economic act—spinning "will turn our faces Godward," wrote Gandhi. His commentary pricks the conscience, as he elevates the "poor sisters of Orissa [who] have no saris; they are in rags . . . they have not lost their sense of decency, but I assure you we have. We're naked in spite of our clothing, and they are clothed in spite of their nakedness."

Having experienced ostracism in South Africa during his years there as an attorney, Gandhi experienced myriad situations in which he was not permitted to function as a human being in the apartheid system—indeed, even in the Christian church. Gandhi wrote, for example, of his admiration for C.F. Andrews and his visit to a Christian church in South Africa to hear him speak. Alas! Gandhi "was not allowed to enter the church . . . because the color of his skin was not white."

A Hindu, for certain, but Gandhi's exposure to and association with Christians, such as Mabel and E. Stanley Jones and Bishop Waskom Pickett, led him to the plain of choice. Also, having studied scripture and writers such as Henry David Thoreau, John Ruskin, and Count Leo Tolstoy, Gandhi wrote to answer Stanley's question about how to reach the Indian. His troubling critique pierces the heart of any thinking Christian:

"I would suggest that all you Christians, missionaries and all, must begin to live more like Jesus Christ. Second, practice your religion without adulterating it or toning it down. Third, emphasize love and make it your working force . . . and fourth, study the non-Christian religions more sympathetically to find the good that is within them . . ."

E. Stanley Jones explained that Gandhi was saying that although Christians don't "reject" Christ, they "reduce Christianity to a creed to be believed, an emotion to be felt, an institution to which [they] belong . . . a rite to be undergone—anything but a life to be lived." Furthermore, he concluded sadly, "we have inoculated the world with a mild form of Christianity so that it is now proof against the real thing."

Mahatma's commitment to ***satyagraha***, a way of life that lives out the "truth force, taking on yourself of suffering, [but] never giving it," mirrors John Wesley's admonishment to do no harm, do good and stay in love with God—so simple and yet so difficult that very few achieve it—whether Muslim, Hindu, or Christian.

Of Gandhi's fasting to initiate change that some, including E. Stanley Jones, criticized as being coercive, Stanley questioned Gandhi, "Does not [your fasting] force an action or result?" Gandhi replied thoughtfully, slowly, "Yes, the same kind of coercion which Jesus exercises upon you from the cross."

Stanley persisted, and wrote Gandhi, "You have grasped the principles [of Christianity], but missed the Person." While this may be true, he also wrote that "Gandhi was a Hindu by allegiance and a Christian by affinity. . . he was more right when he was wrong than we are when we are right. . . he was a natural Christian rather than an orthodox one."

Once Gandhi's resolve had set as rigidly as concrete, he announced his "Quit India" campaign. "This is open rebellion . . . I conceive of a mass movement on the widest scale possible . . . Imprint it on your hearts . . . let every breath of yours give expression to it. The mantra is: 'Do or Die.' We shall either free India or die in the attempt."

Yes, hundreds of thousands *would* die.

While Stanley supported the pledge of the Indian Congress to refuse the British offer for negotiations on British soil, Mabel did not always echo her husband's political understanding. "The Mohammedans [Muslims]," she said, "are keeping out of the present movement and are frankly critical of Gandhi [a Hindu] and his schemes. [Among them] there is, too, a more openly expressed contempt of the Hindu . . . because of his idolatry . . . " as opposed to Muslim worship of one supreme being.

Tragically however, while many Hindus passionately desired home rule, they were encouraged to believe that once " . . . English power . . . [wanes] . . . Christians will be driven out. We have only one religion—Hinduism." In addition to general resistance of British colonialism with its religion [Christianity], the civil war between Hindus and Muslims also escalated.

Although not always successful on the surface, Gandhi repeatedly challenged the common people—all Indians—to, without violence, show the British that they meant business. As an example, only seventy-nine people began the march to the sea to "make salt," the manufacture of which was forbidden by British law. By the end of the march within three weeks, in spite of the ridicule of the British, tens of thousands of protesters convened at the seaside—and the whole world knew it.

Violence of astounding proportions ensued—never intended by Gandhi. The years of civil unrest unnerved all who fought and waited. To some it appeared that Gandhi's methods had been forgotten. Even Mabel, a respected friend of the merchants and officials in Sitapur, experienced a terrifying confrontation.

One day as Mabel drove to the bazaar for supplies, the unruly crowd, supposing the white woman to be British, surrounded the car, rocking it and shouting, "***Mahatma Gandhi ki jai***," translated as victory to Mahatma Gandhi. She frantically searched the faces for a familiar face, but the crowd had gathered from out of town. Mabel began beeping the claxon horn, keeping time to the rhythm of the chant. Its loud hoarse noise amused the crowd. Someone shouted, "Even a foreign car is for independence—but it has a cold!"

Finally and fortuitously, one of the merchants on hearing the ruckus recognized Mabel and jumped onto the hood, shouting that she was an American missionary from the mission station, and not English. "And the crowd parted and in good humor let her pass, still laughing at her horn's chant. A crowd can be fickle, but her quick thinking saved the day," Eunice praised her mother.

In an 1877 portrait, Queen Victoria sits stolidly on her Indian ivory throne after being named "Empress of India." Although she never stepped onto the subcontinent that was her "jewel in the crown," she was so named to inform the Indians that the British were in India to stay. Not surprisingly, the Bengalis, for example, staged massive protests and boycotts of British goods long before Gandhi began his campaign. While India had issued its Declaration of Independence, translation into reality would take twenty years, and even it did not end the violence.

Although the mission was spared disastrous results, millions would drown in the blood bath that washed over India in repeated waves. What was happening in India would affect all of humankind, from Martin Luther King to the young daughter of Mabel and Stanley Jones whose worldview was being shaped by these cataclysmic events.

Chapter 6

Burra Din and a Gracious Giver

Sharing is the very genius of Christianity.
—Mabel Jones

Although the world around her struggled with justice issues, Eunice lived her early years somewhat unaware of the inhumanity and ignorance of discrimination and political upheaval. Her first best friend Bhulan, the Muslim cook, carried her about before she could walk, teaching her to speak Urdu and Hindustani. Eunice credits her world-view with a life-long acceptance—rather than mere tolerance that too often is touted as the ideal—of the influences of her Indian and global connections. She not only early learned Christian stories from her mother, but also Hindu epics and Muslim narratives, replete with their own rich, ancient history and religion.

While practices of segregation and discrimination continued to spread their pall over India, at the same time the people were renowned for their hospitality. Stories abound that affirm the good qualities of both Muslims and Hindus.

It is said that the practice of Muslim's courtesy and hospitality is such that if two arrive at a door simultaneously, they both insist that the other enter first, until alas—neither enters. Also, a Hindu fable tells of a god and a stranger arriving at a gate at the same time. The revered stranger—not the god—is invited to enter first.

Mabel often experienced the kindness of the Indian people. One night when checking the compound, she walked along the back fence where she saw a large pile of rubbish. As she paused to consider what should be done with it, a woman called out and pointing to the stones, she said, "Just before you came, a poisonous snake crawled in among those bricks. I know your God will protect you, but it is just as well to be careful."

* * * * *

Celebration of Christmas on the mission brought joy to all: Muslims, Christians, Hindus. Although money was scarce, and snowmen and Christmas trees, shopping and cookies were hardly an option, one could not escape the impact of this ***Burra Din***—a great day.

Mabel with her teachers and children decorated the classrooms with colored paper and cloth flags. Gifts of tops, whistles and mirrors thrilled the younger children. "You would be surprised to see how much joy a boy can get from a half-cent toy," she wrote the supporters, while a Bible or a hymnbook captivated the boys who could read. "I never knew them to be so happy. I wish you could have seen their faces shine as they received the books so reverently but so joyously. . . and when they were dismissed, they jumped and danced and sang and laughed aloud . . ." Although the books or Bibles were all alike, each one thought his book was the best, and tried to show off its treasures to his friends.

A genuine Santa, Mabel had also prepared a box of school bags, locks, handkerchiefs, erasers and pencils, along with a few toys for the non-readers. But only the toys remained after each chose his gifts. "The poor have a different sense of values," Mabel explained.

A Christmas gift of five dollars from Miss Nellie Logan allowed Mabel happily to purchase six white shirts and cloth for six pairs of pants. She did the cutting; the boys did the sewing in time for their special day to join the church. Another year Mabel described "a rather meager Christmas" for her boys, but they did not complain. One of the older boys told her, "When people are starving, sweets would be bitter in our mouths."

On Mabel's first Christmas Eve alone, indulgence in self-pity tempted her, but by Christmas morning she joined her boys who could not go home, or like many, had no home at all. After breakfasting with them on curry and whole-wheat pancake, the celebration at the mission began.

The Indian children, most of whom had never owned a cent of their own, spent frugally and sacrificially. One boy who received the sum of fifty cents for Christmas from a supporter in the States, faithfully gave one cent in the offering each Sunday until it was gone. What joy he experienced in his ability to give! Another boy bought peanuts every Saturday with his Christmas money and gave them to a five year-old orphan, keeping just one or two for himself. "Often," Mabel wrote, "I accept a new child [into school] on faith, and wonder for days whether the Lord really wants me to go in debt for him. But help always comes . . . Money may be 'filthy lucre,' but here, it is more often like manna from heaven."

One Christmas Mabel made cornucopias with pages torn from *The Christian Advocate*, and filled them with peanuts, Indian candy and a card. Some returned the card, asking to exchange it for a picture of Jesus, having seen some of the little cards typically used in Sunday schools in the States. Even her Muslim cook returned a "gorgeous red and gold card" Mabel thought would delight him and instead begged for one of the "plain little pictures of Jesus."

Without fail early on Christmas morning the schoolboys came caroling what they had practiced for weeks in English. Mabel tried to discourage the practice because of the cold weather at that time of year, but they would not be dissuaded. The Joneses invited teachers, American and Indian, from Isabella Thoburn College in the big city of Lucknow to join them for Christmas. When the carolers arrived, the house guests all struggled from their warm blankets to greet them, handing out fruit and strong hot tea for the adults and weak tea for the children—if the cook had managed to boil water over the charcoal fire.

After children from the girls' school came caroling, presents were exchanged—"which, of course, was my big event," recalls Eunice. A hearty breakfast followed, interspersed with the steady stream of visitors arriving to greet them on Burra Din. The merchants sent woven trays laden with oranges, guavas and bananas for the boys' school.

Church service followed—about a half mile from the mission bungalow. Leaves from banana trees, in the absence of evergreens, decorated the gates of the church, the compound and front of the school. The children flitted about like butterflies as they decorated with yards and yards of colored paper ring garlands they had created.

Three hours later, following a sermon in Hindustani preached to the men and women seated on separate sides of the church, they emerged, the men and women dressed in their best ***kurta-pyjamas*** and saris. Non-Christians also joined the crowds, usually Hindus. Joyful greetings and camaraderie pervaded everything, blurring all differences.

Back at the house, more visitors from the non-Christian community arrived, all expecting a monetary gift if they had served in any capacity through the year, waiting patiently in a long queue. Mabel took time to distribute medicines to ailing visitors, Christmas or not. Following a short rest for the guests, the compound community gathered for the party. When home, Stanley organized the games, and Eunice participated in them all, especially badminton. Lacking tennis balls, the English troops had created this game by sticking a feather into a champagne cork, and naming the game after Lord Badminton.

Then came the fun of opening and dispensing the barrels of used clothing, saved for this day, sometimes with hilarious results. One man chose a pair of wool long johns, the old-fashioned kind complete with its back flap. This he donned immediately over his cotton pyjamas and shirt and was instantly the envy of those who had not spied it first—to the great amusement of Eunice's parents and houseguests. They all indulged in ***jalabis*** and ***gulab jamins*** from baskets bulging with fruits and Indian sweets.

By Christmas evening, all anticipated the long-awaited feast. Mabel often invited single English officials who were lonely so far from home at Christmas. The Muslim cook usually prepared peahen; the peacock tended to be tough. The official Christmas bird in India, it was off limits for the Hindu, to whom the bird is sacred. Occasionally venison was available, depending on successful hunting by British officials. A favorite was Hunter's Beef, again not eaten by Hindus, but considered a delicacy devised by the British who missed their Christmas hams. The cook rubbed a ten- to twelve-pound roast with spices, salt and vinegar and marinated it for several days. Then it was placed in a large ceramic container and sealed with a one-inch thick crust of whole wheat flour ***atta*** (dough). Carried to the local baker, it was baked slowly for several hours. The tasty result reminded them of ham, extraordinarily delicious, and no threat to religious taboos of the Muslim cook who excelled in preparing this recipe.

For Mabel, a bag full of mail from home completed Burra Din. Some were dated as far back as September, and books from Miss Nellie for Eunice were draped in scraps of paper and dangling ribbons after having been censored during war-time restrictions. But her joy overflowed.

Festivals intrinsically comprise religious celebrations. The favorite Hindu festival is ***Diwali***, the Festival of Lights, with Lakshimi, the goddess of wealth, presiding. It is like New Year's Day when accounts are closed and the new year begins. The ***Sikhs***, Parsees and Jains celebrated their unique religious days. For the Muslim the most significant is Id at the end of ***Ramadan***, the month of fasting from sunup to sundown. The proper time to start the fast is in early morning when a white thread can be clearly identified as white. The fast is broken in the evening when the white thread can no longer be identified as white. Or, an amusing tale the Muslims tell on themselves is that one could also go to a cliff and shout across the valley, "Shall I keep Ramadan or No?" And the answer, of course, echoes in the wind: "No! No! No!"

Needless to say, at the Sitapur Methodist Mission, Christmas Day celebrated the Savior's birth, a Burra Din. Well respected, the day overflowed with joyous greetings from their non-Christian friends: Burra Din Mubararak Ho! Eunice anticipated Christmas all year, and as she grew she came to understand its significance for herself and for all persons.

Eunice faithfully wrote her own childish thank-you notes for gifts received. One to Miss Nellie read: "Thank you very much for these nice books. I like them very much. I got fifty presents and yours now makes fifty-two and some more are coming. Don't you think that is a good deal for me? I hope you have a happy new year."

* * * * *

The modern missionary movement did not introduce Christianity to India, and in fact some suggest that Apostles Thomas and Bartholomew came from present-day Syria to the Malabar coast in southwest Kerala State in India and established a church. Although the legend has not been proven, the evidence is strong. While the Orthodox Church for centuries was isolated and ingrown, in the twentieth century the Mar Thoma (St. Thomas) Church experienced a great spiritual awakening and is considered the evangelistic arm of the Syrian Orthodox Church.

Among Eunice's fondest memories was attending with her father the annual Mar Thoma Christian Convention in South India. E. Stanley Jones not only attended regularly, but also preached for them, wearing, as they do, the traditional white robe. Between 75,000 and 100,000 persons attended these gatherings, held outdoors beneath a palm leaf ***pandal*** on poles, on the sands of a river bed in Maramon that was dry in winter and a roaring river in summer. The palm leaves were expertly woven to create the huge shelter. Because they did not have a public address system, men were stationed at every grouping of five thousand people to relay what they heard. Stanley gave them their first public address system, and on his 80th birthday, the Mar Thoma people gave him an exquisitely carved ivory box depicting the convention site and audience as well as the prominent loudspeakers. The box remains one of Eunice's most meaningful treasures.

As a young person after meeting the leader, Father Abraham, Eunice remarked that if Jesus were living on earth today, surely he would look like and be like Father Abraham. "His demeanor is so inviting; his robe and beard so white." He radiated a sense of the holy.

* * * * *

Visits to the States were rare. On Mabel's first furlough, Eunice was two years old. As a result of the war, the voyage took five to six rather than the usual three weeks. Clayton, Iowa, hugged the banks of the great Mississippi where her beloved grandfather had willed to Mabel the cottage he had built. Here Eunice, quite the curiosity, met her extended family for the first time. Although Eunice understood but did not speak English on arrival, she soon learned to speak it when she discovered that no Hindustani was spoken or understood in Iowa.

Attending church as a two year-old, Eunice caused not a little embarrassment to her mother. Mabel already knew that her little daughter would be best confined in a place where everyone knew her—in the cottage. Friends of the family, many of whom were German Lutherans, invited Mabel and her cute little girl to attend their church where Mabel's relatives were members.

Mabel warned the minister, "It's too difficult with my daughter. She's only two years old."

Oh no! I'd love to have her," he assured Mabel. "She doesn't bother me at all."

Finally, when Mabel's sister visited with her children, they attended the church together. One mother put her foot up at the end of their pew, and Mabel put one foot up to block Eunice from escaping at the other end of the pew, but they did allow her to run back and forth between them. Eunice thought this great fun. Suddenly, she ducked under one leg and ran forward and behind the pulpit where the pastor was preaching away. Peeking between his legs she called to the congregation, "Peek-a-boo!" Some parishioners were aghast, and the minister never invited Mabel to return with her daughter. Mabel told Eunice that she was known as "the heathen child" by some of the townspeople, many of whom thought the incident amusing. The pastor did not.

Of the two stateside visits before starting college, Eunice was nine years old on her second visit. She remembers that journey across the seas when the family spent several weeks in Jerusalem at the American Colony, started by the Spafford family. Anna Spafford had set sail for Europe with their four daughters. Horatio Spafford planned to meet them later.

On Anna Spafford's fateful journey, the vessel sank and the children drowned in the icy Atlantic. Rescued, Mrs. Spafford wired her husband, "Saved alone." He left immediately to sail across the ocean to mourn with his wife. Staring incredulously from the ship into the dark depths, Spafford saw where his children had died with 222 other persons. Retiring to his cabin he wrote the beloved Gospel song, "It Is Well with My Soul," illustrating the faith that fortifies the believer through the most paralyzing and devastating experiences of life.

When peace like a river attendeth my way,
When sorrows like sea billows roll,
Whatever my lot, thou hast taught me to say,
It is well, it is well with my soul . . .

* * * * *

On arrival in Dubuque, Iowa, Eunice was ready for her first

experience in an American public school, remembering it with great pleasure. She made many friends, but recalls that her strange accent prompted teasing by classmates who laughed at her because she "spoke like a book," much too correctly. "I soon tried—and succeeded—in learning all the slang I could, much to my mother's dismay," Eunice recalls. At home in the neighborhood on a steep hill in Dubuque, Eunice honed her skill at maneuvering on roller skates without breaking a bone.

One wealthy woman who was entranced by Stanley's speaking invited Mabel and Eunice to visit in her massive, extravagant home in Philadelphia. "I still remember the house," Eunice says, "because in it was a true aviary!" The woman's daughter, the same age as Eunice, had recently died, leading to an offer to Mabel to allow her to adopt Eunice.

Believing that the child would be deprived of many material things and opportunities as a missionary's daughter, the woman pled with Mabel, promising, "She will want for nothing if you allow me to adopt her!"

When Mabel rejected the offer, the woman showered Eunice with dolls and other gifts, for which the Joneses had to pay enormous duty. But the saddest part of the story followed with the Great Depression, in which the couple lost everything, and the husband committed suicide.

Years later the woman contacted Mabel, who was on furlough again, wanting to visit her. Although the beautifully attired woman in her grey suit with matching accessories again impressed Eunice, she confided to Mabel that she wore her remaining presentable outfit. The rest had been sold along with her other possessions. In fact, she did not have adequate bus fare to return home. Mabel, of course, bought her ticket. Once again, Mabel and Eunice reflected in awe at Providence that guided them.

* * * * *

Up to ten or twelve years of age, the girls in Sitapur played together, most likely at the homes of Eunice's friends. Then, as the family developed trust of the Christian family, they permitted their young daughters to visit Eunice in her home as well. But once in puberty, the girls left childhood behind—supposedly—and were in ***purdah*** themselves, soon married and with children.

Eunice forged deep bonds with some friends, including one Muslim girl in particular. The woman in Philadelphia who had tried to adopt Eunice had sent her an Effanbee doll that opened its eyes, cried when turned over and had movable arms and legs. It even said mama. The girls dressed and undressed the doll with its own wardrobe and play-acted many a scenario while their mothers visited. When Eunice returned to the mission after her year in the States followed by her first term in boarding school, her old friend sent for her, begging her to bring the doll. Overjoyed to see Eunice as well as the doll, she told her story.

"When I was thirteen, my parents forced me to marry Salim. He is thirty years old," she said. "I do not like my husband. I wanted to die when my baby began to grow inside me."

Eunice cringed. She did not want to hear the details. "But now," the child continued, "I want to hold my little girl, but my mother and my grandmother took the baby from me. They do not let me hold her. They will not let me be the mother. I am my husband's wife . . . but my arms are empty."

"Here, here," Eunice thrust her beloved Effanbee doll into her friend's arms, moved by her friend's sadness. "Please take it. Take it with you. She can be your baby now," Eunice told her, symbolic of her empathy and generosity for a lifetime.

Mabel, too, often felt the pain of the plight of children who became wives and mothers. She once wrote about a child she couldn't help noticing while waiting for the train in Sitapur. When the train arrived, the Hindu girl about ten years old who had been sitting on a box arose and took a few faltering steps toward the train. She then looked up into the face of an old man with gray hair who accompanied her and said something to him. He stooped, picked her up, and carried her onto the train.

Some orphans in Mabel's school in Khandwa.

Above left: The bhisti carrying the pigskin waterbag.

Above right: Mabel and daughter Eunice.

Right: Bhulan, the Muslim cook on right, with the Christian houseboy on left.

Left: Wedding of Eunice and Jim with E. Stanley and Mabel Jones, and attendants Carol Titus and Mabel Wagner.

Martin Luther King talking to Eunice about her father's influence.

Fowey Castle, home of ancestors of Eunice and Mabel.

Left: Mabel being carried through rising flood waters.

Below: Mabel with her school boys lining up for the walk to church.

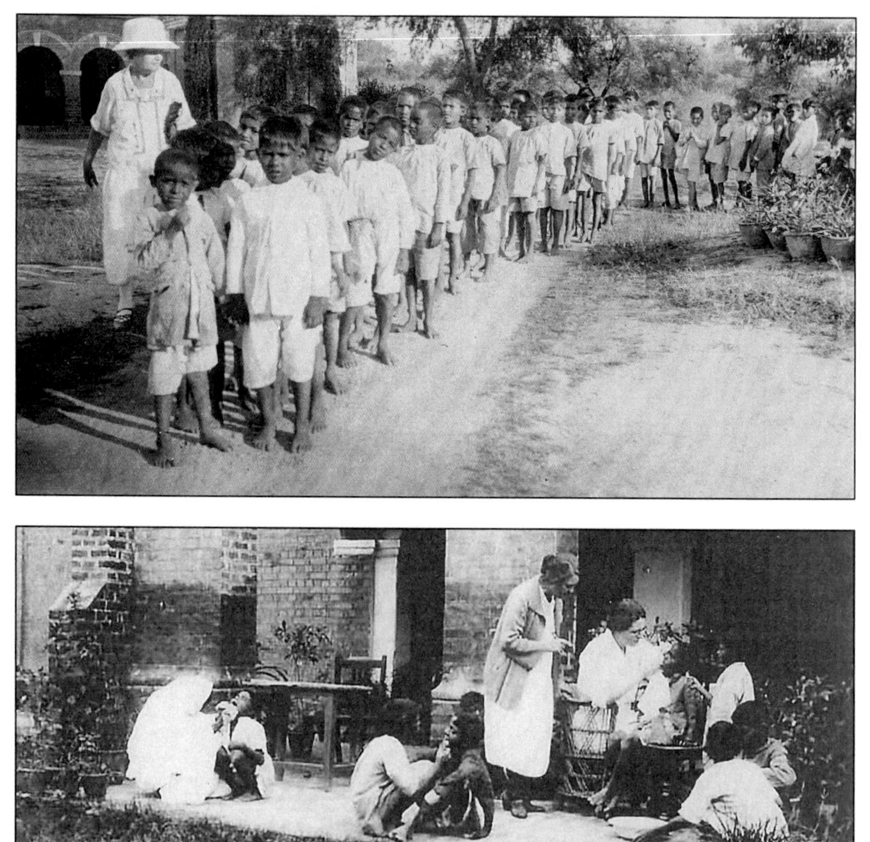

"Doctor" Mabel and helpers treating her students.

Baby Eunice with her parents Mabel and E. Stanley Jones.

Eunice and Jim in traditional sari and kurta pyjama.

Nur Manzil Psychiatric Hospital.

Above: Eunice with her Ayah.

Left: Mabel Jones on her 100th birthday.

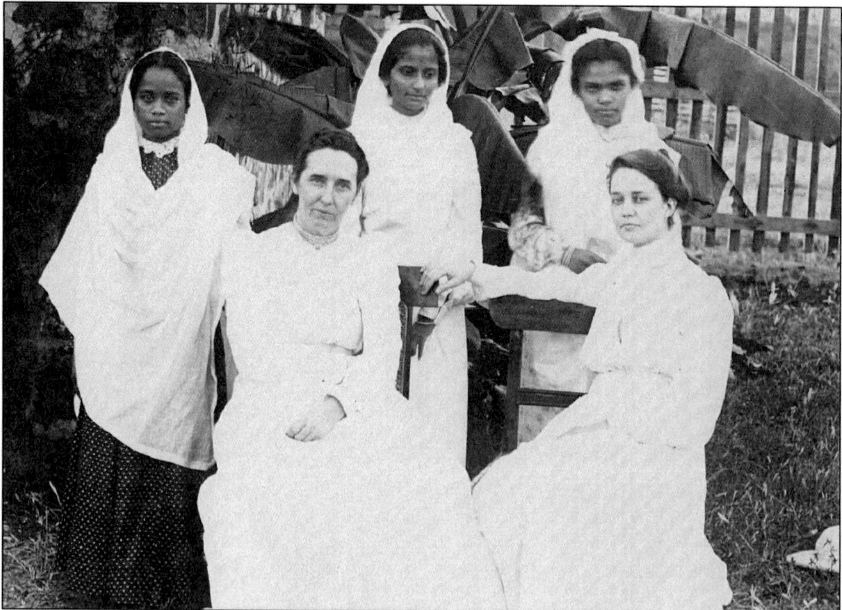

Mabel (right) in 1904 in Khandwa.

Above: Eunice with doll.

Left: Eunice and Bishop Mathews with their three children (l. to r.) Jan, Stan, Anne.

James and Eunice Mathews.

Jan Stromsen, daughter of the Mathews, with her grandchildren Alex and Kate, the great, great grandchildren of Mabel and E. Stanley Jones.

Above: Eunice and friends preparing for a trip by elephant.

Left: Mabel with six of her boys.

Later when Mabel passed his window, she asked if his little girl was all right. Puzzled, he pointed to the child and said, "Her? She's my wife." Her jewels were so heavy on her hands, arms, feet, ankles, even on her face, ears and neck that she could not walk. Mabel returned to her seat with tears in her eyes and an aching heart. "Poor little girl wife!" Mabel wrote. "No more playing with dolls or making mud cakes for her."

Although many Indian laws today help protect women and children from this kind of abuse, it continues. Not only does it affect girls at the onset of puberty, but often it begins before birth as well. For example, Amartya Sen, Indian economist who won a Nobel Prize in economics, coined the term missing women to describe females killed as infants in societies where male children are preferred. In India alone, current estimates of "missing" stand at 50 million, resulting from selective abortion and infanticide.

Paul Jeffrey, United Methodist missionary and senior correspondent for *Response*, stresses the fact that abuses of globalization and technology add to the cultural discrimination against women and children. For example, big business, such as Coca-Cola, have moved into forty-four cities in India, resulting in such atrocities as lowering the water table causing wells to run dry, allowing dangerous pesticides to contaminate the drinks and selling Coke in remote villages where even medicine for children is unavailable.

As recently as 2001, a government census in India estimated that 12.6 million children under the age of 14 work for pennies a day. NGOs suggest a more likely 50 million child laborers, thanks to the demands of imported goods sold in GapKids, Macys, Ikea, Lowes and other venues. Even younger children, 5–14 years of age, account for more than 2.5 million laborers.

Also, the practice of ***dowry***—in which the bride's family pays money and goods to the groom—and reverse dowry in which grooms pay money for a valuable wife—continue to plague India. Other demands on his in-laws by the husband may continue throughout the marriage, often resulting in his beating or burning his wife to produce the shocking statistic of an estimated 15 thousand deaths annually, resulting when the in-laws cannot oblige his ongoing demands for material goods beyond the original dowry price.

Although dowry was made illegal in 1961, Madhu Bhushan, India coordinator of the Asian Women's Human Rights Council says that the law has done little to stop the practice. Also, thousands of widows, often mere children, continue to be ostracized for the disgrace of not having a husband. They are forced to live out their lives, heads shaved, in Hindu temples, with no opportunity to re-marry.

Years ago at an All Women's Conference, Mabel heard Christian, Hindu, and Muslim women, some still in purdah themselves, passionately speak against such practices that continue to bind many in shackles. Even today the Hindu practice of ***suttee*** continues, in which a woman will burn herself to death rather than become the wife of a man who already has a wife.

Laws may change, but tradition dies a slow death.

On their return to India, both Mabel and Eunice faced their impending, inevitable nine-month separation. School in the States had been fun, but boarding school would provide yet another dimension to her education. Little did Eunice realize the differences she would face following her childhood at the mission and her new life in a "Dickensonian" boarding school.

Chapter 7

Wellesley and Woodstock

It takes a village to raise a child.
—An African Proverb

Mabel had struggled with the incomprehensible act of sending her almost-twelve year old daughter on a two-day journey by train to Wellesley boarding school where she would live most of the year. Most missionaries and non-natives sent their children to boarding school. But for Mabel and Eunice who were unaccustomed to separation, the severance would border on amputation—things would never be the same again.

"We had never been apart, and it is not easy to be away from one's only child nine months of the year," Mabel wrote. "But there is nothing else to be done if we stay in India . . . We cannot choose our sacrifices. We are glad that we are found worthy to bear something that is really for His sake."

Eunice recalls that journey to ***Naini Tal***, the closest boarding school to the mission where she had attended kindergarten and lower elementary grades as a day student, when the family climbed the five or six thousand feet to their summer get-away each year. As temperatures soared above 120 degrees Fahrenheit in the shade in the valley, they packed as though for a major move, including pots, pans, blankets, office supplies, everything needed for living for two months, accompanied by a cook and at least one other helper.

Although the two-day train journey was not as difficult as climbing with the horse-drawn cart, this time Eunice and Mabel knew they were packing not for vacation, but for education. Boarding school harbored secret terrors for Eunice, in addition to facing months of separation from her mother.

Of course, Eunice had to leave all her pets at home on the mission. She now recalls that they seldom survived her absence—for reasons unknown to her, at least. While at school, she delighted in adopting the giant beetles that amused her and the other children. Attracted to bright lights, they swarmed in great numbers, and simply by opening the screen door, Eunice welcomed her newest pets. The children named them based on their short pinchers (rhinos), their long, double pinchers (stags), their branched horns (hornos), and the longer, four-inch horns (reindeer). Although they had a vicious clamp, the children "tamed" them by feeding them sugar water, making them "drunk" and harmless. Wearing one of these "pets" on a lapel incited envy in the others.

While Mabel had taught Eunice during elementary years and plied her with books from infancy, Eunice does not recall any formal instruction. The children on the mission were in school most of the time, but Mabel did not force Eunice to attend, much to her regret. Although Eunice spoke Hindustani, she did not learn to write Urdu and Hindi. India has about fifteen languages and scores of religions, but Hindi is now the official lingua franca adopted following Independence.

Naini Tal was a large town with six schools run by churches, one each for boys and girls: two Catholic, two Church of England and two Methodist. The clientele was about the same and included high-caste Indians, the boxwallah—including missionaries and the British who had neither contacts nor resources to send their children back to England, and the Anglo-Indians (British and Indians who had intermarried and remained in India). Curriculum followed the British system with Cambridge senior examinations, and strict Victorian discipline supported by interminable lists of rules. Wellesley students did not wear uniforms as others did.

Named for its first principal in the 1880s, Wellesley was considered a good school, but discipline was purely Victorian. They polished their skills at punishment that supposedly helped children to build character. If one were not adequately prepared for lessons, the consequences could be dire, not to mention embarrassing. A typical punishment was memorizing this or that canto and then repeating it line by line, the child's voice quaking like a leaf in a storm.

"Here it comes!" The girls cowered on the inside while standing at attention on the outside. In any given moment that bony finger could target a racing heart like a laser gun. "A terrifying experience," Eunice recalls. "Give me a verse," the principal demanded. Each girl frantically searched her memory for a verse. The shortest verse in the Bible, "Jesus wept," was not permitted. Eunice still quakes with the mandatory memorization and quoting of Scripture.

For Sunday services the girls marched two by two in a long line to the Methodist Church two miles downhill and, of course, two miles back uphill. "Yes, we were taught the Bible, but I don't think it was real teaching. In the fourth grade we studied kings in the Old Testament. What those kings have to do with me today, I don't know. That didn't help our spiritual life in any way," Eunice said. "We also memorized long lists of dimensions, including those of King Solomon's temple," she lamented. "What they taught did nothing to develop our relationship with God and others. I learned that—I suppose—by osmosis from those around me, including my mother and father. Even back in the mission church, the language was high Urdu, terribly boring to me."

To complicate eleven year-old Eunice's relationships with these diverse groups in boarding school, while Indians accepted her, the English considered boxwallah to be lower class, including missionaries. Also, most students had been boarders from kindergarten, while Eunice had attended the lower grades only occasionally in the summer. She was further disadvantaged by being one of three Americans in the school—one in kindergarten and the other a non-boarder. Accustomed to diversity on the mission, discrimination shocked Eunice, especially as she suffered the full brunt of it. The Anglo-Indian girls, themselves victims of discrimination, chose to scapegoat the Americans. Not only students, but also many Anglo-Indian teachers threw barbs at the Americans—primarily Eunice.

As Eunice explained, "Who was there to receive it? Me." She still shivers to recall those years, remembering them as extremely traumatic and, she says, "I have tried to shove it all into the back of my mind." Although her mother was a friend of the principal, Eunice can only remember the experience as out of a Dickens novel.

Even the British nurse, referred to as Sister, intensely disliked Americans because she had served in World War I where she had come to despise American servicemen. Eunice dreaded any contact with the nurse, because she delighted in humiliating her with her sarcasm. "Here comes our American. I know she has no bravery about her!" she taunted Eunice.

"I couldn't talk to the teachers or principal about this—or my mother who was two days away. But my parents had taught me well. I was not a whiner!" Eunice reminisced.

One day Eunice fell and scraped her shin. "Rather than go to the infirmary, I said nothing and it became badly infected, so I wore black stockings to hide it. But one day the principal noticed my limping," Eunice said.

"What's wrong, Eunice?" she demanded.

"Nothing."

"Come with me," the principal said. She insisted that Eunice pull down her stockings, then instructed her to report to the infirmary immediately.

"No! Please, I don't want to go," Eunice begged her.

But she insisted, and Sister vented her anger on Eunice for not coming earlier. Eunice's feeble excuse—not the real reason—did not satisfy the nurse. She scraped the area thoroughly without using an anesthetic as Eunice bit her tongue and allowed her to clean and treat it. Suddenly, Sister looked at Eunice with a new kind of respect. Perhaps her conscience pricked her. But all she said was, "Well, I have finally found an American who is brave!"

"Maybe you noticed I've been very tough on you," she told Eunice, "because I loathe the Americans. I got to know them when I was sent to nurse a battalion of American servicemen in World War I. I'm very glad to find somebody who wasn't like them," she said. "Now, tell me about you, about who you are and why you are here."

"She completely changed her attitude toward me and was very kind," Eunice remembered. Whether or not the nurse learned anything, the child Eunice learned the lesson well, valuable knowledge that would help shape her worldview. For whatever reason, people struggle with pain, prejudice, mistrust . . . but a personal relationship can bridge the chasm, no matter how deep or wide. So, British nurse and American schoolgirl linked in friendship.

The only boys in the school enrolled in kindergarten before being transferred to the boys' school for grades. When one of the little ones had an accident, the principal tied a pot onto the child's head to teach him to hold his urine. "Terrible! The poor child had to walk around with this wretched pot on his head, which didn't help one bit. It likely exacerbated the problem," Eunice reasoned.

No one had a private room, and beds in the dormitories were lined up head to foot in long rows. If a child needed to go to the bathroom at night, she climbed a hill of fifty steps or so to a line of commodes. Possibly the only perk the girls enjoyed was permission to visit the home of a day student on the last Saturday of the month. What nearly spoiled the privilege was what awaited them on their return. The nurse always lined up glasses of Epsom salts mixture that she forced them to drink to ward off any disease or infection. It may have worked, but more than once the potential "cure" also worked better than iron bars or rules to keep them inside—it often wasn't worth a few hours' escape.

Happiest when she could leave boarding school for vacation at home, Eunice waited one day with others at the train station. Suddenly, a boy she had previously met rushed up and practically threw two of his white mice to her. They were of kindred spirit, and Eunice knew he liked her, but did not realize he cared enough to part with two of his precious mice.

The teacher had not seen the transaction, so Eunice, all smiles, quickly concealed them inside her jacket and buttoned it snugly. Through the long journey she slept with the furry creatures cuddled inside her warm coat. When they arrived about three o'clock in the morning, Mabel asked Eunice why she kept her coat so tightly wrapped around her. Surely, she must be ill. A Sitapur summer hardly calls for a coat.

The little creatures found their new home quite comfortable and set up housekeeping in a dresser drawer with many clothes in which to burrow. Eunice fed them well and cleaned up after them. Or so she thought, until one day Mabel noticed that all Eunice's little folded dresses had holes, all in the same place. It looked as though someone had drilled a hole through the whole stack. Speechless when confronted, with no easy fabrication at hand, Eunice confessed. The mice were released into the great out-of-doors where they quickly disappeared.

* * * * *

In 1930, at Stanley's insistence, his sixteen year-old daughter transferred from Wellesley to Woodstock. Mabel preferred that Eunice complete her secondary school education at Wellesley, but Eunice was delighted with the possibility of attending a coeducational school based on American curriculum with well-trained American, Indian and British teachers.

Located in Landour in the Himalayas, in the hill station of ***Mussoorie***, Woodstock became the mecca for American missionary children of all denominations, as well as some English and Indian students, including Parsees, the Zoroastrians of Persia. Known for caring for one another, few Zoroastrians knew poverty. Eunice was invited to weddings of a number of students of different sects and religions. It never occurred to her that to some people, different meant wrong.

Although based on American schools, they also offered British Senior Cambridge to those who preferred it. But there were no more long lines by classes to events. No more rows of beds by classes in large dormitory rooms. No climbing the steep and endless steps to the long row of commodes at the top of the incline in the dark night. No more marching in long lines to see an approved movie in town. Woodstock was as free as Wellesley was not. Eighty years later, Eunice still reports, "I loved it!"

The girls even had cubicles with a shared bathroom between them. Eunice considers herself blessed and fortunate to have shared the unit with Grace Cansick, the daughter of British missionaries. A match made in heaven, the two treasure their nearly eighty-year friendship, still corresponding and telephoning across the Atlantic. Grace became a nurse and married a doctor. "Woodstock gave her to me!" Eunice says.

Mary Thomas, another Indian friend, was daughter of Chief Justice (Sir George) of the High Court of United Provinces where the mission was located. A Christian and Methodist, Lady Thomas became close friends with Mabel. Their daughters played together from about the age of four. Mary became a medical doctor and married Billy Badhwar, a nominal Hindu educated in England who later served as head of India Railroads. During their decades of friendship, Eunice, first alone and later with her husband, stayed with Mary and Billy whenever in Delhi.

During summers, some children joined their parents in apartments, rented houses or stayed with friends. Eunice once stayed with a family whose girls walked more than 500 hundred feet down to their school. Their watchman lived in Bhotya near Tibet, and one day he brought his wife, about the age of the teen-age girls. To them, he looked like an old man of about eighty, though he likely was not more than forty. Unhappy with her husband, she tried to avoid him at night when he became amorous, sometimes climbing a tree to escape his advances, while Eunice and her friends slept on the verandah.

One day the younger daughter of the missionary family got chicken pox, and before long the three teen-age girls picked it up. All were miserable. The watchman's young wife massaged the girls because they ached all over. When she didn't appear one day, the watchman told the lady of the house that his wife ached all over. She gave him Ellerman's Horse Liniment with its wonder-working power on sore muscles. A few days later she returned, looking perky.

"What are you doing still sick?" she asked the three teenagers. "Why didn't your mother use what she sent with my husband?"

"Well, that is for backs, not chicken pox," they told her.

"Yes, I know. I had the same thing you did. I got bumps all over, so my husband put me on the floor, sat on me, and rubbed the Ellerman's into all my sores. The next day they were gone. See, I have no more chicken pox. What about you?"

Speechless, what could they say?

* * * * *

Stanley's Christian ***ashram*** was located about twelve miles from his family when Mabel and Eunice lived in Naini Tal in the mountains during the two summer months, allowing them to spend more time together. Although twelve miles meant a long walk, they appreciated the proximity.

When Stanley was able to spend time with the family, they treasured the joy of it. Always playful, he once staged a mock wedding, posing as the "bride" with a basket of vegetables as the bridal bouquet. Eunice adored her too often absentee father.

Stanley insisted that his daughter excel in sports. "I think he was disappointed that I wasn't a son, but he determined to teach me everything a boy could learn." Eunice reasoned. She described her father as very athletic. He taught her to play tennis and badminton—not considered women's games in that era. When women did play, they served underhand, not overhand. "My father refused to acknowledge that sexist rule," Eunice laughed.

Stanley did not like the British caste system any more than the Indian caste system. The British had their club in Sitapur, but he did not feel at home in it. Instead, he frequented the Indians' club where Hindu and Muslim lawyers, doctors and other professionals met evenings for tea and tennis. Eunice was his regular partner and they often won. Initially disapproving, the men soon adjusted their blinders. They couldn't help it, because Eunice played tennis so well.

Not only her father, but also the boys and teachers at the mission were always ready to play games, including field hockey and badminton. At home Eunice played some of the students' rough games, such as ***kabadhi***, an Indian game with four thousand years of history that now has global followers. Played by two teams of seven each in twenty-minute halves, it's all about self-defense, attack and counter-attack. The field is about half the size of a basketball court.

The boys also taught her to fly kites, and Eunice became an expert at it. Far more than running with the wind, their game included "cutting" another person's kite by putting ground glass on the string. A competitive art, the goal was to cut an opponent's string as the sky filled with soaring kites. Suddenly someone's kite would flutter down . . . then another . . . and another.

Again, Eunice excelled in her game, but she admits, "I don't think Mother ever knew. She would never have allowed me to do that. It was too dangerous. There were a lot of things [the boys] let me in on that Mother didn't know," Eunice laughed as she recounted it. Eunice's friends included the somewhat guarded relationships with Indian boys at the school before she began boarding school. She enjoyed the Indian children on the compound as well as the Hindu and Muslim children of the more educated and well-to-do families who lived nearby. Only the men were educated, for the mothers were in strict purdah, their bodies fully covered and separated from men and strangers by a screen or curtain. Mabel got along well with those women in ***zenana***, and took Eunice with her to visit them.

Although walking was the primary means of transportation, at times other means sufficed. Not until the 1920s was a car available for Stanley's work, used on occasion by Mabel. Even then, roads had not been developed in many of the places Stanley traveled, so he utilized train, bicycle, or a ***dandy***—a box-like conveyance carried by four people in the mountains—or a variety of carts pulled by a horse, pony, camel or ox. A more exotic means, such as the silver chair atop an elephant on which Stanley rode at the coronation of King George V, provided a capacious view, but Mabel much preferred anything but the elephant for herself. She did permit Eunice to climb onto an elephant sent occasionally to pick her up for a play-date with the daughter of an Indian ***rajah***.

Eunice still treasures the days when she and Stanley took long hikes together into the fields and villages adjacent to the compound. "We often walked five miles, passing through villages where the people always welcomed us. Indians are very hospitable," Eunice reminisced. "Never did we enter a home without being offered something to eat or drink."

"On those walks my father taught me about many religions, because in some ways my life was a bit isolated," Eunice said.

"When we passed burning ***ghats*** in villages along the banks of the Sarayan River, my father explained that Hindus burn their dead bodies, while the Parsees expose dead bodies to scavenger birds. This differs from the Muslims who bury their dead," Eunice recalled. Stanley extrapolated on traditions and customs and cultures, attempting to introduce an expansive worldview. Her father wanted her to understand that each is part of the whole.

On their meandering walks when they came to a stream, he'd say, "Jump, Eunice!"

Eyeing the challenge, she sometimes responded, "I can't!"

"Then fall in!" he'd chuckle as he continued walking.

"With that kind of training," Eunice explained, "I grew up knowing negativity had no place, because Daddy would have no part of it. I can hear him saying, 'If you can't do it, pay the consequences.' That I consider good teaching!" Eunice attributes her athletic activity and years of hiking and walking in the Himalayas as the foundation for her current good health as she nears the one-century milestone.

* * * * *

Having completed her education in India, Eunice knew her father had been right to advise her transfer from Wellesley to Woodstock. Despite her mother's objections, Woodstock had helped prepare her for the transition to college in the United States after graduation in 1932. There is no doubt that the imprint of the subcontinent also prepared her for a life of service, unlike her mother's, yet reflective of deep resources common to both women.

Eunice was about to embark on a new journey into a life unimaginable for most children of India—including this child of India.

Chapter 8

Watching God Work

We know that all things work together for good
for those who love God . . .
—Saint Paul

As the parallel lives of Eunice Treffry Jones and James Kenneth Mathews almost imperceptibly begin to converge, the reality of God-at-work resembles the finger of God in creation as depicted on the ceiling of the Sistine Chapel. No less awe-inspiring is tracing Providence in the lives of these two choice persons.

1930–1933

Mabel and Stanley attend the Central Conference where they elect Jaswant Chitambar as the first Indian bishop. It is during this time that the Indian Congress declares its independence from British rule, another significant milestone that initiates years of turmoil and bloodshed before it is realized.

But Eunice is ailing. In her senior year of high school, the doctor considers her fatigue, weight loss and general malaise to be harbingers of a "nervous breakdown." Mabel's concern leads her to demand x-rays that reveal three wisdom teeth impacting nerves that appear to be the culprit. Also, Dr. Butcher—that same doctor who delivered Eunice—diagnosed a recurrence of tuberculosis, likely because of its prevalence in India, but that Eunice today reasons was erroneous conjecture. However, acting on this life-sentence on her daughter, Mabel leaves the mission to spend ten days with Eunice when hospitalized, and then several months more as she convalesces. Finally, Mabel urges Stanley to come home to take Eunice to Switzerland to recover. But as he prays, he is assured that Eunice is recovering. The doctor confirms the good news, telling them that no sign of tuberculosis is apparent.

Meanwhile, recognition as a scholar marks James Kenneth Mathews' last year in high school. Known as Ken at home and school to avoid confusion with his father with the same name and known as Jim, his after-school work includes three jobs. The Great Depression hits hard, and Ken works for a year before entering college. Intending to save money for school, he instead helps support his family with every cent earned.

1933–1937

Following graduation from Woodstock in the winter of 1932, Eunice, like Ken whom she does not know, has a ten-month reprieve before beginning college. Mabel sails for Europe with Eunice and her friend Nancy Moffat, also the daughter of missionaries, where the girls study French and Italian for college credit at the Crandon Institute in Rome, a school sponsored by the Woman's Foreign Missionary Society.

They often hear Pope Pius XI address the gathered thousands from the balcony in St. Peter's Square, and frequently listen to Benito Mussolini speak on his balcony in the Piazza Venezia. Receiving tickets to many cultural and religious events at the Vatican, the girls are soon showing off the splendor of Rome to American tourists.

En route to the States they stop in Switzerland to visit friends in the Alps, until at last Lady Liberty welcomes them home. One British passenger exclaimed, "Well! She's fat!" Mabel later wrote: "Well, perhaps she is fat, but no graceful, slender Venus, no far-famed marble statue in the Vatican . . . or the Louvre of Paris ever gives us the thrill that comes when we sight this motherly matron who welcomes us home." Yet she sadly writes that much of India that she leaves behind continues to be "poor, hungry, naked, poverty-stricken, idol-worshiping, caste-ridden, God-searching . . ."

Once home, Stanley meets Eunice and Mabel for a much deserved month of relaxation at the beach in Ventnor, New Jersey. But soon Eunice begins coughing again, perhaps adjusting to the climate change. Mabel, too, experiences more problems with her throat, necessitating cancellation of speaking engagements.

But at last Eunice begins Oberlin College in Ohio with her attentive mother in a nearby apartment. Ever watchful, Mabel writes her intent to settle Eunice in a college "where she will keep well physically and morally." She refuses to leave Eunice where "halls of the best girls' dormitory are blue with cigarette smoke . . . or where the professors . . . raise doubts of everything we hold sacred, but do nothing to solve those doubts; or where one is sneered at if she goes to Sunday School and church—or doesn't approve petting . . ."

Both mother and daughter not only feel the stress of health issues, but disappointment with the United States, particularly with many young people they encounter. One young woman, scantily attired, blows cigarette smoke into Mabel's face while "talking of sex in the language of a doctor-book." The girl smirks, "I suppose you're dreadfully shocked, aren't you?"

"No," Mabel replies. "It's rather hard to shock one who has spent over half her life in a land where women and children smoke as a matter of course; where children are clad in smiles and sunshine, and the peasant wears only a loin cloth to cover his nakedness; where men and women and children speak frankly of the most intimate details of life. But I am puzzled over two things:

Your attitude, if you consider all this right and proper, [and] why, as Asia becomes more Christian and what we call "civilized," these customs tend to disappear; but in this supposedly Christian and civilized land we are reverting to the East."

Mabel also wonders at the rationale of those who say they cannot give money for mission, yet are still "attending movies, buying trivia, eating out, and using their cars for pleasure trips."

In that academic year, Eunice diligently practices hours each day on piano and organ as she studies for the six-year major in music. But one year is enough to confirm that music is not her first choice, but her mother's. She transfers to American University, a Methodist school in Washington, D.C. In one of her classes, the students reach consensus after much discussion: The greatest contemporary Christian leader is E. Stanley Jones. The Rev. Dr. Ray Wrenn, then one of Eunice's classmates, recalls that class with Eunice and his amusement at her reaction. She unsuccessfully tries to hide from the class both her embarrassment—and pleasure.

During that same time Ken Mathews works diligently, supporting himself in college, following a pre-med track, intending to become a surgeon. His intense schedule limits social interaction—again. In retrospect, he sees the hand of God clearly, such as in the days he lay unconscious after hitting his head on a stone after diving into a river. Expected to die, not only does he survive, but his journey stretches before him in a whole new trajectory. Influenced significantly by his brother Joe and other companions on the way, he experiences genuine conversion and a call to ministry.

1937–1939

Following graduation from college, Ken begins seminary. Quite unsuspecting, he attends a service on an October evening in 1937 in which Bishop Azaiah of South India preaches. So it is that, like the unexpected bombshell that re-directed the life of Mabel Lossing in Iowa in 1904, another explodes in 1937, catapulting James K. Mathews towards India. Mathews knows instantly that he will go to there as a missionary, likely following seminary. But the next morning at the chapel service in Boston University School of Theology where he is a student, the secretary of the Board of Foreign Missions of the Methodist Episcopal Church mentions that a pastor is needed in an English-speaking church in Bombay.

Within three months the twenty-five year old Mathews sets sail for India, leaving his theological training in the dust for nearly twenty years. Although he meets an appealing young woman on board, once again, God has better plans for his future. Mathews settles into his new appointment as pastor of Bowen Memorial Methodist church in Bombay, named for the beloved American missionary George Bowen who, once he set foot in India, never left. Young Mathews welcomes to his city church such influential visitors as Georgia Harkness—and E. Stanley Jones.

With close friend Paul Wagner, Jim journeys on church business to ***Sevagran***, where Mahatma Gandhi's ashram is located. As the young men set out for a walk one morning, they notice a small, brown man with walking staff emerging from the gate of Gandhi's home and ashram. Cordially, the revered Gandhi invites Jim and Paul to accompany him and others on their morning walk.

"Who are you?" Gandhi inquires of the two men.

"We're Methodist missionaries," they said.

"I thought so," Gandhi said.

Then he shocks them with a question.

"I wonder whether, if John Wesley were alive today, would he recognize you people?"

During Eunice's senior year at American University, Stanley tells his daughter that he wants her to travel with him as his secretary for the next year. "We've spent years separated; I've traveled and you've been in boarding school and college, so it's time we get better acquainted," he tells her. He wants her to be useful, however, so, following graduation in 1937 she begins a secretarial course that includes shorthand and typing at Baylor Secretarial School in Dubuque, Iowa.

Such a simple thing! Such an inconsequential course meant only to fulfill her father's wishes! Such a mundane pursuit! But it would lay the foundation for service for at least the next seventy years.

Before Eunice completes her course, Stanley calls on her to attend the National Christian Preaching Mission to Universities with a team of well-known, distinguished, ecumenical participants. Not only does she act as secretary to her father to practice the skills she's learning, but also, before long, such noted scientists as Arthur Compton, winner of the 1922 Nobel Prize for Physics, and eleven others in the group begin dictating their speeches to Eunice. She excels even though some of the "southern-speak" challenges her understanding, as well as accuracy and speed in meeting their demands to return their typed manuscripts: "Pronto!"

Although already impressed with her father's writing and preaching, one night Eunice finds herself in the crowd packed into Madison Square Garden in New York City where Stanley is to preach. She recalls Stanley's meetings with highly educated, often non-Christian listeners in India where she had tried to dismiss her girlish terror when he opened meetings to questions after a lecture. Sliding down in her chair, wanting to hide, she'd thought, Oh no! He can't answer that! But he always rose brilliantly to the occasion. Hearing him speak at Madison Square Garden convinces her yet again of his ability.

Stanley leaves the U.S. while Eunice completes her courses with plans to meet her father in China in 1938, but the war between Japan and China is horrendous. Stanley barely escapes the carnage known as the Rape of Nanking, in which Japanese kill 150,000 Chinese, rape thousands, and execute soldiers. Plan two develops: India is substituted for China.

Again, Providence leads the two young people toward an intersection. Back in India at last, Eunice helps her mother at the mission and also spends time in Stanley's ashram in ***Sat Tal*** where she assists her father.

With the revenue from sale of his books, Stanley had initially bought 450 forested acres at about 5,000-foot elevation in the Himalayas to establish a Christian ashram in 1930. Of Sanskrit derivation, shram means hard work. The prefix can mean a negative, or an intensive, so that the ashram is both a place where work ceases, and also where the intensive work of prayer begins. Time spent in an ashram includes reflection, Bible study, preaching and hard labor, a combination that reflects the life of E. Stanley Jones.

Stanley welcomed all, both Christian and non-Christian, to Sat Tal's large house and several cottages, all of which he later gave to the Methodist Church. Described as a "vacation with God," the ashrams grew like bamboo throughout India, the United States, Europe, Japan, Africa and Latin America.

1939

Stanley is scheduled to preach and teach for a week in Poona, while he and Eunice stay with a missionary couple there. Known as a matchmaker, the woman gushes about a young man who also is coming, and even informs Eunice that he is the one for her. Eunice tries not to show her annoyance, but even before she meets this stranger, she refuses to entertain any interest.

The young pastor of Bowen Memorial in India has exchanged the moniker Ken for the name Jim. Within a short period of time, in spite of having fallen in love with India, Jim nonetheless feels a great sense of loneliness saturating his days and nights. He welcomes an invitation to travel by train to Poona to hear the well-known evangelist E. Stanley Jones preach.

Orchestrated by his friends there, the visit will include an informal visit with their guests staying with them: Dr. Jones and his daughter Eunice. Jim says of their first meeting that he was "smitten when Eunice walked into the room and into my life." Although Jim does attend Stanley's lectures, he and Eunice quickly carve out time to bicycle and even tour the countryside in a borrowed car. More dismayed than surprised, Jim learns that other young men have shown interest in Eunice, including British officials offering proposals.

Back in Bombay, busier but lonelier than ever, Jim begins a

letter to Eunice in the formal manner of that cohort: "Dear Miss Jones." He later learns that her father had to assist in deciphering his scrawl, much to their amusement.

While intensely hoping for an answer to his letter, Jim decides to return to Mahableshwar for another month of uninterrupted language study, having already begun studies in the Marathi language. Spoken crisply and written in script similar to Sanskrit, Jim finds it daunting. So when he receives an invitation to attend E. Stanley Jones's Sat Tal ashram for that month, he does not need to pray about the decision. His plan for language school dries up and blows away on the winds of desire to see Eunice again. What he does not know is that the intense schedule at the ashram, with both Mabel and Stanley watching every move, will somewhat cramp his style. But the friendship blossoms.

On a couple of afternoons away from the ashram, Eunice and Jim hike or ride horses to Naini Tal where Eunice had attended Wellesley. Anyone unfortunate enough to drown in her lake is considered an offering to the Hindu goddess Naini. The spectacular view of 25,000-foot Himalayan peaks draped in snow stamps itself indelibly on the psyche. On one memorable visit, Eunice's horse throws her onto the narrow trail. But the joy of massaging her painful back with that British remedy, Ellerman's Horse Embrocation—that works equally well on man, woman and beast—pleases Jim. Eunice, incidentally, does not care to recover too quickly. All too soon, May passes and again they separate.

Three months pass before they meet again for a week in Bombay, and by this time Jim drops the formal address—one would hope so after the Ellerman's Embrocation intimacy! Eunice travels with her father for another preaching series in Bombay where Jim still pastors, and where Eunice's parents had been married in that same church.

1940–1942

In January the two meet again, this time in Sitapur, where Eunice gives the grand tour of her childhood home on the mission and the community.

They next meet in Lucknow where Jim plans his agenda. The time is now. Stanley goes for a haircut, and in that safe and private environment—private because the barber speaks only Urdu—Jim pops the question to his would-be father-in-law.

That day, with her parents' blessing, the two visit a German Jewish refugee who had fled Hitler and settled in Lucknow where he opened his jewelry shop. Of course, Jim has to borrow money for the ring that he pays back after selling his typewriter in Bombay. He likely recognizes that the secretarial skills of his new wife will negate forever the need for his own typewriter. Within twenty-four hours, the jeweler fashions the ring that has symbolized for nearly seventy years the everlasting mysteries of love and of God-at-work in their lives.

On June 1, 1940, all eyes follow the bride as she appears to float down the aisle toward the altar with its picture window that opens to the garden. The Belgian Catholic sisters in South India created the net veil and white gown with threads of silver shimmering through its gossamer loveliness. Stanley and Mabel "give away" their only child to James K. Mathews in the teak-paneled chapel of Wellesley School in Naini Tal in the Himalayas. Bishop John Wesley Robinson and Eunice's father perform the ceremony in the presence of Indian and missionary friends. With eyes only for each other, the couple today barely remembers the reception that follows.

Morning finds them on their way to Kashmir, often called "the loveliest place on earth, an emerald set in pearls." Mabel had once written from Kashmir when she had escaped the unbearable summer heat in the valley, "I never expected to reach Paradise without dying, but I feel I am there now . . ." That British subjects could not own land in Kashmir did not dissuade them from building palatial houseboats. The couple, hardly isolated from the world as they'd intended, greet dozens of other missionary friends vacationing on the lake.

Honeymoon or not, life in a houseboat ranges from simple to

elaborate, but even their simple houseboat rivals the dreams of most vacationers. With an attached cookboat, servants and ***shikari***—a small paddleboat for side excursions—the couple is served meals on the roof. The ***wallahs*** climb aboard and tempt them with such luxuries as fruit, flowers, silks and carvings. Amazingly, the honeymooners' simple houseboat and its amenities cost nine rupees per day, about three U.S. dollars.

All too quickly they must disembark and return to Bombay. It is said that the attendance of young Indian and Anglo-Indian beauties declined when their pastor showed up with his lovely new bride. A friend rents a room with them, providing just what they need to afford an apartment near the church. Eunice quickly endears herself through her hospitable entertaining and quality work as secretary for Bishop J. Waskom Pickett.

Mabel joins the couple for the Central Conference held in New Delhi. The trip allows time to visit Old Delhi with its antiquities, such as the Red Fort with its gardens and marble fountains and baths carved in the shape of flowers that sprayed perfumed water in its prime. Jim and Eunice cover the nearly five thousand mile round trip back to Bombay on a "zone ticket," providing unlimited travel for three weeks at a cost of five dollars.

By this time, the three years to which Jim had agreed to serve in India calls for a return trip to the States—with his bride—to return to seminary. Instead, Bishop Pickett appoints Jim as district superintendent of a rural area of the Bombay district. His travels to distant outstations often leave Eunice in charge of much district work. Together they complete that fourth year.

* * * * *

When World War II is declared, like World War I it hits with cyclonic force. Even though England and Germany sign a mutual treaty to prevent war, Hitler breaks the contract, and Europe cowers under repeated bombings that precipitate full-scale global involvement. Its sticky web intricately enmeshes the newlyweds.

Once again the trip home is cancelled, this time due to the war. On December 7, 1941, the Japanese attack Pearl Harbor. The preemptive attack shocks the world and pushes the United States to declare war against Japan.

Struggling with pacifist views, Jim nonetheless concludes that he has no right to "hide behind the cloth" and must do his part. When he hears that a U.S. Army contingent has arrived in Delhi to make preparations to use India as a conduit to supply the beleaguered Chinese army under Generalissimo Chiang Kai-shek, he travels to Delhi to offer himself as a chaplain. He is informed that he would need to return to the U.S. for training. However, someone with knowledge of the country and its people is urgently needed, and he is asked whether he would accept an assignment in the Supply and Quartermaster Corps. Jim agrees to the newest adventure.

Lt. General R. A. Wheeler commissions him on the spot as an officer and assigns him to the port of Karachi, where over the course of the war thousands of American troops would disembark to start their overland journey across India to northern Assam. There supplies are ferried by air across the Himalaya mountains, known as "the Hump," to China, a perilous venture. More than six hundred U.S. planes are lost on this dangerous journey, flying over the Hump day in and day out, with no letup for inclement weather, monsoon deluges, or the Japanese Mitsubishi A6M Zero fighter planes. With Burma—now called Myanmar—and the Burma Road largely under Japanese occupation, and with the new treacherous Ledo Road still in progress, this airlift is a vital lifeline.

Eunice joins Jim in Karachi and is immediately assigned to a secretarial post at headquarters. As her illustrious reputation for secretarial skill spreads, her assignments vary. When an enlisted man assigned as court stenographer has a "nervous breakdown," Eunice is requisitioned to replace him. Much of her work as court stenographer demands verbatim reports of highly classified court martial cases.

During one of the court martial trials, the young defendant uses an expletive that Eunice writes phonetically, with no idea of its meaning or spelling. Pronouncing the word as she heard it, she later she asks Jim about the unfamiliar word. He is aghast. "Where on earth did you hear that?" he asks her—and he educates the gentle woman.

When the new Office of Strategic Services (OSS), forerunner of the CIA, sets up an office in Karachi, Eunice is assigned to their office. To this day, Eunice has not divulged the information to which she was privy while in military or OSS assignments.

Then Jim is sent to Chabua, Assam, and Eunice obtains a transfer to Chabua where she is again assigned to headquarters. They are fortunate to find rooms on a tea estate for living quarters off-base. Jim finds his work both demanding and challenging as he oversees shiploads of supplies arriving from the United States, arranges their shipment further north, and deals with local merchants for necessities of the U.S. troops arriving in India. Jim finds that supervising the ferrying of cargo over the Hump is equally challenging in Chabua. Though not a designated chaplain, in the course of his four years in the China-Burma-India (CBI) Theatre, Jim performs baptisms and burials, celebrates the Eucharist and counsels the troops.

After the war the CBI Theatre became known as the Forgotten Theatre, but it was a vitally important resistance to the rapidly advancing Japanese venture in southeast Asia, clearly an essential component in the war with Japan.

* * * * *

Back at the mission during this time, Mabel finds that the vital connection of support through the mail is detoured and censored, sometimes arriving months later and stamped, "Damaged by being submerged"—under red tape? Food is rationed and other goods, like fabric, trickle slowly into the hands of merchants who further inflate the cost.

In spite of deprivation, Mabel writes that during Lent her boys always want to sacrifice something for their Lord. "Often it is a lump of sugar they receive only on Sundays, or the meat they are served twice weekly, or [eating] less to save flour they can sell to help the poor on Easter Day." Her answer to a questioner shows her dedication to and even admiration for the children. When Mabel is asked, "What is your hobby?" she answers thoughtfully, "Boys, just boys."

Uncharacteristically, Mabel writes in 1940 that "America looks good to us these days. It seems to be the only land left where one can live unafraid. What the future holds, who can prophesy? There is so much to worry and perplex. There will probably be much more in the days to come, but we are in God's hands."

1943–1945

Even after the war, not much changes. Some of Mabel's boy-soldiers return from Japanese prison camps with horrific tales of atrocities. One tells her, "Only faith in God kept us from going mad. Twelve of us met every night for a prayer meeting and, as we had no Bibles, we repeated the verses we had learned in school from memory." Mabel listens with both great sadness and profound gratitude.

Stanley had flown to the States after Eunice's wedding to honor speaking engagements, not knowing he would not be permitted to return for four years. His friendship with the nationals made him suspect, resulting in refusal to grant a visa.

Meanwhile, Jim serves in India another ten months after the war. Even this is fortuitous, because he has been appointed to serve as Secretary of the Burma/India region by the Methodist Board of Foreign Missions. As yet, Pakistan is still part of India. While waiting transport to the States amid the post-war scramble, Jim wisely uses his time to acquaint himself even more fully with the mission work to prepare for his position as Secretary. Of course, he causes quite a stir when he shows up on mission stations and in churches in full military dress, as he has no presentable civilian clothing. Jim recalls it as the "least expensive mission secretary tour on record," still on U. S. military duty—with no duties.

No longer can one just hop a boat for anywhere, just for the asking. Although Mabel is packed since March, she finally arranges to sail on a freighter with seven hundred others leaving in early May, but ends up in a Calcutta hospital diagnosed with "a tired heart." At last she does arrive in the States in August 1946, leaving her heart behind after having served forty-two years in India.

Gazing back over their shoulders, Eunice and Jim see the hand of Providence. Then they turn to look ahead by faith, farther than the human eye can see. With profound thanksgiving, they watch God work, prodding, shaping, blocking, opening doors, closing doors, using the right people at the right time . . . as when Jim divulges a secret to General Wheeler.

Chapter 9

Fingerprints on the World

You must be the change you want to see in the world.
—Mahatma Gandhi

At Army headquarters in New Delhi, General Raymond Wheeler, who had commissioned Jim in 1942, inquired about Eunice. When told that she was pregnant he said, "I will give this my immediate and sympathetic attention." Sympathetic because travel back to the States, other than for the military, was a complex ordeal during the war. Deciding she should give birth in the States, the general arranged for high priority transport.

Dressed in army khakis and carrying Jim's duffle bag with its Army insignia, Eunice began a rough ride to the airport. Twice, she was bumped off flights because they were already full—once in Karachi, again in Casablanca—but each time, she was hustled onto a plane as soon as someone learned she was carrying "high priority" orders from the general.

By the time she reached LaGuardia Airport in New York—several days late, in spite of General Wheeler's orders—the young pregnant wife looked like she felt: walking in a fog of total exhaustion, hungry, sleep-deprived, and terribly rumpled. Jim was in Karachi, Stanley in Alaska and Mabel still in India. Eunice had no U.S. money to make the long-distance phone call to Montclair, New Jersey, but a kind young G.I. called Jim's sister for her. Never having met her brother's wife, Elizabeth had no idea who "Jim" was, because the family still called him Ken or Kenny. But eventually Eunice made her relationship understood and made her case for needing a place to stay.

Hailing a taxi to take her to the bus station, Eunice was astonished at the driver's reaction. "A hero!" he exclaimed, noticing her attire and Jim's army duffle bag. Extraordinary joy and accolades greeted WW II returning military. Full of questions, the cab driver learned more about Eunice and suddenly understood she was on the way to meet her new family. Aghast, he gave her the once-over and exclaimed, "Girl, you look like hell! You can't meet your new family looking like that!" He even offered to take her to his wife where she could re-coup—New York cabbies at their best!

Jim's sister Elizabeth did welcome her, but when Eunice's doctor cousin, Howard Jones, returned from overseas military service, Eunice moved in with him and his wife, also a physician. Georgeanna Seegar Jones, known for starting the first in-vitro clinic in the United States, worked at Johns Hopkins Hospital, where Eunice gave birth to Anne on April 17, 1946.

Today a clinical psychologist, daughter Anne works as Director of the Division of Prevention, Traumatic Stress and Special Programs under the U.S. Department of Health and Human Services. Like her grandmother, Anne is committed to an initiative to reduce/prevent violence, foster healthy development and provide mental health services for children.

Also having completed graduate studies from Wesley Seminary

in Washington, D.C., Anne Mathews Younes edited and compiled for her dissertation fifteen choice sermons given to ashram retreat groups by her grandfather, E. Stanley Jones. Eunice deciphered many of Stanley's sermons from his rough notes and outlines, as he did not prepare them in manuscript form. The sermons Anne used were all transcribed from recordings made by different individuals at some of the ashrams. The dissertation was published in 2008 as *Living the Way: Selected Sermons of E. Stanley Jones on Self-Surrender*, accompanied by recordings of Jones delivering those sermons, now transferred to CDs.

* * * * *

Jim's appointment as Secretary of the Burma/India region dictated their need to live in New York City, the headquarters for the Methodist Board of Foreign Missions. Given the post-war rush on housing, everyone knew that finding a place there was impossible. But Eunice's quiet prayers and listening ears led to a phone call about an apartment soon to be available near Columbia University. Eunice planned to see it the following day.

Traveling by train to the city, she transferred to a subway marked Morningside, heading toward 54 Morningside Drive. She found herself, unfortunately, on Morningside Avenue downhill from Morningside Drive—way, way downhill. A policeman noticed Eunice looking for the number and offered to help. He could not hide his surprise. Warily, he pointed to the street at the top of the slick hill. Not to be outdone by weather conditions—or her seven-month pregnancy—Eunice crawled up the icy hill, mostly on her hands and knees.

What a prize! The woman was magician Harry Houdini's sister, who not only wanted to rid herself of the two-bedroom apartment with one and a half baths for five thousand dollars, but also the furniture as well. Eunice bought the furnishings for five hundred dollars, including the chairs on which Houdini had sat many times. As Eunice was not ready to move in until Jim arrived to begin his new work, she called the Board office to tell them she had bought it. Not only were they amazed, but also delighted that she was willing to rent it, fully furnished, for six months to another Board employee who needed a six-month lease. Once again, Eunice watched God work, far more dependable than weather conditions or Houdini-magic.

The apartment was across the street from the home of the president of Columbia University, Dwight D. Eisenhower. During the time that Eunice and Jim lived there, Eunice daily climbed to the roof to hang up baby diapers to dry. There she had a clear view into Eisenhower's studio. Stripped to the waist, the future President of the United States often retired to his penthouse to paint, having been encouraged in this pursuit by Winston Churchill. Eunice often watched his artistic endeavors, and her visitors, in exchange for the view, would ever so slowly help her take down and fold the laundry blowing in the evening breeze.

While living in New York City, Jim walked to Columbia University nights and Saturdays to fulfill requirements for his Ph.D., all the while working full-time and traveling as Secretary. In fact, Eunice obtained permission to sit as his proxy in classes when Jim was on the road. She took notes in shorthand and typed them for his later perusal.

Since he had missed the birth of his first daughter, Jim determined to be home for the birth of his second daughter, Janice, born in New York City on November 9, 1947. While growing up Janice spent more time with her grandmother Mabel in Iowa than did the other grandchildren. "She taught me how to enjoy spending time on my own and to figure out how to do things for myself," she fondly described those treasured days.

Jan Mathews Stromsen attributes her independent nature to her grandmother and mother. It may explain the unusual positions—particularly for a female—in which she has served, both inside and out of the federal government: Deputy Chief of INTERPOL and Director of the International Criminal Investigative Training Assistance Program (while serving in the U.S. Department of

Justice), and as the Vice President for International Programs within the non-profit National Center for State Courts. All these positions involved travel to developing and/or post-conflict countries, such as Haiti, Liberia, Bosnia, and Kosovo, to work on re-establishing police or other justice sector institutions.

Like their mother and grandmother, both sisters live "to serve this present Age, [their] calling to fulfill."

Jim's work as Secretary of the Burma-India region soon led to other opportunities, providing a forum for his and Eunice's ministry which neither one would have dreamed possible. Their connection with and understanding of the global village not only sent them to every state in the U.S., but also to every continent, except for Antarctica. But India continued to run like a vibrant thread through both warp and woof of Jim and Eunice's tapestry.

Among the opportunities was preparing for mission the Methodist J-3s (Japan-3), a precursor of the Peace Corps. These young, short-term missionary groups, rather than individuals, were recruited and trained before being sent to a country in South America, Africa, Japan or India for a three-year service term. The I-3s (India-3) sent to India/Pakistan, for example, participated in an intensive six-week training with emphases on theology, Indian religions, Asian art and music, Christianity and Communism, Indian Christianity, and an introduction to Urdu and Hindi. About forty young recruits experienced Indian food, dress and culture and visited the United Nations where Admiral Chester Nimitz briefed them on the Pakistani struggle.

Also while serving as secretary for India and Burma, Jim was elected to the broader position of Associate General Secretary for missions, now known as General Board of Global Ministries (GBGM). Then, as chair of the Methodist Committee for Overseas Relief, now the United Methodist Committee on Relief (UMCOR), Eunice and Jim watched in awe to see its powerful impact on global suffering from natural or man-made disasters. Having experienced the war years, they had already grasped the vital impact of giving through UMCOR. Among other places they intersected with 280,000 refugees from the war that resulted in the independence of Bangladesh from West Pakistan.

Another connection with the world led them to Japan where they were part of a gathering of leaders of international ecumenism. Eunice and Jim hung spellbound to every word of the Reverend Takyo Matsumoto. Having been principal of the Hiroshima Girls School when the United States dropped the atomic bomb on that city, he recounted the moment when the school with its eighteen teachers and 350 girls disintegrated instantly. Yet he spoke of a new future, echoed by Board Secretary Diffendorfer who challenged the listeners to "create a world in which atomic bombing will have no part . . . . Humanity stands at the parting of the ways . . . one road leads to the universal Christ . . . to peace within a world community of brothers. In the other road stands Black Chaos . . .the way to war and to the suicide of civilization."

While Eunice traveled with Jim whenever possible, she was also fully occupied with parenting three children, often in Jim's absence. Having outgrown the little apartment in New York City, they had moved to Montclair, New Jersey, to a house from which Jim commuted. Eunice had formed close, congenial ties with spouses of other ecumenical Mission Board Secretaries. Like her, many had been born in or served in other countries, so they shared common backgrounds and needs. Eunice characterized their camaraderie as a relationship with "new names, new jobs, but the same need." The women strengthened and supported one another in ways that oftentimes the sisterhood knows how to do best. They stood strong—and sometimes alone—as necessary. Eunice's model in her mother Mabel proved helpful for that kind of testing.

Having sometimes experienced similar, though not as extended, separation from her husband, Eunice understands the complex reasons for frequent geographical distance for her parents, Mabel and Stanley. One need only look at the demands of world wars, extreme transportation difficulties on both the subcontinent and globally, the unique qualities of both Stanley and Mabel and, above all else, their agreement from the beginning of their relationship that their calls to ministry would trump other desires, including spending time under the same roof.

Stanley revealed his deep pain about his absence from Mabel and Eunice in India. Stranded in the states during World War II, as a pacifist Stanley worked for peace between Japan and the States, all the while preaching, teaching and writing. International travel restrictions between India and the United States on all except medical and military personnel not only prevented Stanley's return, but also his decision to "abandon public neutrality on political issues" resulted in his being refused a visa to return to India during the war.

Yet ironically, the British secretary wrote Stanley after the war that independence had been achieved "by the grace of God and such help that you and others have so graciously given." Stanley said of the fiasco: "[They] kept me out for standing for India's independence, and then thanked me for help in achieving that independence."

* * * *

Bishop Susan Morrison describes Eunice as "the last of Methodist royalty." More than a reference to her ancestral history and those with whom she rubs shoulders, this description embodies a woman whose life exudes the aura of one who lives life in being as well as in doing. "It is not I, but Christ within me . . ." is her mantra. Rather than a right bestowed by human birth, Eunice counts royalty as the birthright of every person who humbly yet confidently claims by faith a relationship with Jesus, elder brother, son of God. But Eunice's earthly "royalty" also deserves a closer look.

Maternal—and Methodist—ancestors of Mabel and Eunice were of Cornish descent from the town of Fowey on the southern coast of England. Eunice proudly carries Treffry as her second given name. When the Treffry castle in Fowey was attacked by Bretons intent on revenge for an attack on their ship by Fowey fighters,

Thomas Treffry was not at home. But his wife Elizabeth, courageous as the women who would follow her in the twentieth and twenty-first centuries, saved the castle by pouring boiling lead from the tower onto the heads of the assailants—hardly like Eunice whose courage takes her in other directions!

The Treffry's son John was knighted at Bosworth on his return from exile with King Henry after being forced to leave the country for joining the proclamation of Henry as King. Centuries earlier, according to Mabel's report, her ancestors can be traced to William the Conqueror, a wise ruler, "a man of temperance and devout religion." One of Eunice's ancestors attended the coronation ball of Queen Elizabeth I.

Eunice with her husband once visited the Treffry castle. Not having made prior arrangements to visit, it did not appear accessible until Jim noticed a huge gong with a rope that he promptly pulled, resulting in a frightening boom that echoed around them. In short order a woman elegantly dressed appeared and questioned their presence. Embarrassed, Eunice searched for words until, wanting to interject some humor into the situation, Jim said,

"She's your long-lost cousin!"

"Well . . . what branch?" questioned the suspicious woman.

Again, Eunice was speechless, but finally blurted out Grandfather Treffry's Christian name: "John!"

They were graciously invited inside and corresponded for years.

Migrating to Ontario, Canada, in the nineteenth century, the Treffrys moved next door to the Lossing family, Quaker immigrants from Holland. John Lossing married his neighbor, the aristocratic Emma, who rode her horse side-saddled. When townsfolk saw her riding, they called out, "Here comes Lady Lossing!"

The couple moved to the States, crossing the Mississippi and settling by a waterfall in Clayton, Iowa. Emma died young with tuberculosis, but lived long enough to give birth to Mabel Lossing's father, Charles. As a skilled carpenter, John built the house that would become the treasured possession of his beloved granddaughter Mabel. As John did not have a studio, to showcase his skill John created nine different styles of doors in the house he built for himself. Customers could view the doors in his own house as a sample of his work, assisting them in their choice of a style for their own house.

One of those doors, wider than the others, was a "coffin door," wide enough for the passage of a coffin into the house for funerals that were commonly held in the home of the deceased. John Lossing's funeral was held in the house he built.

* * * * *

Mabel arrived in the States to stay in 1946, and settled into life away from the subcontinent where her heart would forever feel most at home. News of the turmoil in her beloved land of India rocked her to the core. It had been a long time in coming, but come it did.

Finally, the British agreed to "Quit India," and on Independence Day, August 14, 1947, the Constituent Assembly of the Government of India climaxed its session with the tolling of the clock, the deep-toned "oooom" of a conch shell to "call the gods to witness some august occasion." Outside, rockets soared and fireworks boomed. It was "Times square on New Year's Eve," wrote a *Chicago Daily* correspondent. Nehru's grand summation pronounced: "Long years ago we made a tryst with destiny, and now the time comes when we shall redeem our pledge."

But it was bitter victory, for with independence came division. Independence created two countries: India and Pakistan. Under the unyielding demands for a separate Muslim State, Mohammed Ali Jinnah and his militant Muslims had won the partition of India: parts of western, northern and eastern India, with majority Muslim populations, would now be Pakistan—"Land of the Pure." Pakistan itself later was truncated when the eastern section withdrew and Bangladesh was born.

India, even after partition into three countries—Pakistan, Bangladesh and India—has the second largest Muslim population after Indonesia. Hindus number about 75 percent and Muslims 15 percent in India. Christianity is considered a "foreign" religion, although refuted by E. Stanley Jones in *The Christ of the Indian Road.*

From across India dire reports squelched further celebration of Independence. Violence broke out in Calcutta with refugees fleeing the city as Muslims, now in what they considered hostile territory, fled toward the "Land of the Pure." In one day "there were 4,700 dead, 15,000 injured, and 150,000 refugees fleeing the city."

In equal numbers, Hindus and Sikhs, whose ancestral homes were now in a foreign and hostile country, fled toward India. From "Lahore came the report of 153 dead and scores of buildings ablaze, including 5 Sikh temples and 23 shops . . . Amritsar, too, was under siege, and smoke rose above hundreds of ***Punjabi*** villages." Also from Calcutta came word of a "bomb explosion and the [ironic] discovery of stockpiles of arms in the area where Gandhi was fasting to end the killing."

Gandhi was frequently asked about his fasting and other non-violent acts of persuasion. What should a non-violent person do when confronting anyone, whether relative, friend, even other countries? "The first step," Gandhi patiently explained, "is gentle and affectionate persuasion. When it fails . . . voluntarily [one] invites suffering in his own body to open the eyes of the person who is determined to see no light."

When Gandhi wrote the eight conditions on which Muslims and Hindus must agree or he would fast to the death, he staked his life on their acceptance. His extraordinary commitment asks: "Are my method and my aim right? If so, the consequences are in the hand of God." Gandhi's actions and words were one. Any student of history, however, can see that actions—however lofty the intent—can become the means of destruction and death. Indeed, "What difference does it make to the dead, the orphans, and the homeless," asked Gandhi, "whether the mad destruction is wrought under the name of totalitarianism or the holy name of liberty and democracy?"

According to Bishop J. Waskom Pickett, at partition millions clogged the country in the frantic two-way exodus that included 783 refugee trains, and thousands by ship and planes. Those traveling by land convoys were subject to the worst, including starvation and ambushes. Along the rail line into Delhi, bodies piled up on either side of the tracks for fifty miles like flotsam . . . bodies . . . human beings.

"No fewer than eleven million Hindus, Muslims and Sikhs crossed borders, which to this day remains the single largest episode of migration in history." Refugee camps sprang up like wild mushrooms in the night. Unbelievably, nature joined the desperation of pilgrims as the monsoons swelled five rivers in Punjab, adding to the horror and suffering with an unstoppable downpour that saturated not only the refugee camps, but also the rivers, causing the worst flooding in their history.

Procuring potential volunteers for the refugee camps added to the dilemma for the fledgling Church World Service camp, formed after the world wars. Why would Sikhs, who had just murdered more than a thousand Muslims, volunteer their assistance to the injured? Why would the Muslims lend a hand to their potential murderers? However, the courageous response of the Christian Indians begs description. They somehow filled the gap in 160 camps, many of which were tent cities, one in ***Humayun's tomb***, a mausoleum. For victim and volunteer, one wrote that "the old tomb became the saddest place on earth. Not knowing one another's language, grief was the real lingua franca among the refugees."

Bishop Pickett attempted to wire the Methodist Mission Board for help. They needed tetanus, penicillin and antigas gangrene serum. "You want medicine to save these damn Moslems [sic]?" the telegraph operator shouted incredulously. "Let them die!" The fledgling Methodist Committee on Relief, precursor of UMCOR, valiantly attempted to respond to needs.

"Ethnic cleansing," a term that described Hitler's Germany and

Gandhi's India, was at work without naming it thus. To all appearances, everyone hated someone, and all paid the price. "Do or die!" had been the battle cry. Unfortunately, they got both: Independence insured that the bonds of colonial rule were severed at last, but this led to wholesale slaughter among Muslims and Hindus and others.

A night visitor begged Bishop Pickett to visit Prime Minister Nehru to help him realize the danger that Gandhi courted. Nehru already knew that an attempt on Gandhi's life had been thwarted. He had tried, but Gandhi had not been persuaded to move to safety. "Will you go to Gandhi yourself?" the visitor begged Pickett.

The clock was ticking. Within minutes, a frail but smiling Gandhi surprised Pickett by meeting him at the door of ***Birla House*** where he was fasting. For three quarters of an hour Pickett attempted to persuade Gandhi to move to a safer location. "Why should I be afraid to die?" he asked. "All my hopes for a better India are being destroyed. Perhaps Gandhi dead will be more respected than Gandhi alive."

Heavy hearted, Pickett reported, "I failed completely." On the evening that Mahatma Gandhi was shot by a bullet fired by one of his own Hindu people, hushed crowds waited outside Birla House where they had carried him. Finally a secretary came out and brokenly announced to the stunned masses: "***Babu*** is finished."

But the world knew better. On the day in which independence was proclaimed, a cartoon had appeared in the ***Amrit Bazar Patrika*** in Calcutta, picturing an infant India, entitled, "Great Expectations." But the shadow the child casts is Gandhi's.

The news had not yet reached Pickett, but two days after his conversation with Gandhi, a young secretary approached Pickett at a meeting and tearfully informed him, "Mahatma was shot and killed."

Prime Minister Nehru requested Pickett to speak for Christians at the memorial service. Pickett also conducted a memorial service for students at the Isabella Thoburn College. "Gandhiji was not of an age, but was for all time," Pickett told the crowds. They sang a favorite hymn of Gandhi's, "Lead Kindly Light" by John Henry Newman.

Lead, kindly Light, amid encircling gloom,
Lead thou me on!
The night is dark, and I am far from home . . .
Keep thou my feet;
I do not ask to see the distant scene; one step enough for me . . .

* * * * *

Long before Eunice's birth and even before Mabel's years at Sitapur, she had reflected on the changes in her Pollyanna attitude as India absorbed her into itself.

"Every journey needs a journal," says Phil Cousineau. Fortunately, we can join Mabel on her life-journey for a century through her writing. Mabel not only kept meticulous financial records throughout her adult life, but also wrote stories for children and adults and preserved time in her newsletters and journals. This entry shows the change in perspective as her eyes adjusted from the tourist-lens to reality:

"Three years ago I sat here on this verandah . . . and my eyes fell on the same scene, but how different it all looked! Then I saw, but knew not. India seemed like a land of poetry; the people like big simple-hearted children; the tumble-down huts of mud and straw, quaint and interesting; the white tombs and altars under the green trees, picturesque . . . . India is still interesting—I want more than ever to live my life here, but it's no longer a fairyland. The charm of the fading green trees, the gorgeous blossoms and luxuriant foliage is broken and I would change the whole yard full to see a maple tree putting on brilliant colors of autumn, or an oak tree with its bare branches or a simple spring wild flower. . .

"The sun used to appear like an old friend. Morning after morning I stood in my door to watch it rise. But though I do that now sometimes, it is not with the same love and delight, for I cannot but remember its cruelty during the summer when its rays were like a flame's heat, and we fought it with tactics and punkahs and barred doors. I know how many a child has met death and how many an older person has nearly lost his life by its fierceness. Even when it is in good behaviour [sic], we dare not step across the lawn without a pith helmet to protect us from his arrows . . .

"But don't think I'm unhappy here, or that I have ceased to see beauty in the world of nature that God has created for India . . ."

Mabel hardly accepted that her work was complete just because she had retired after forty-two years in India. So skillful she was at writing letters, that at age ninety Mabel was still raising money to support her boys in India. In fact, her letters that presented needs by way of stories about the students rather than directly soliciting money, generated such phenomenal financial revenue that Secretary Diffendorfer of the Mission Board had asked her to prepare a model for other missionaries. That she did. Her son-in-law Jim wrote of her that she "did not have an abundance of possessions, but rather a paucity of needs."

After her return to the States, Mabel spent some time in the old home place in Clayton, Iowa, where books had filled her childhood home. There she had taught her first students—her younger siblings—and read until she "cried from sheer weariness and grief because [she] had to stop." It was there that she began the writing that became an integral part of her persona.

While still a teen-age girl, Mabel had experienced her greatest loss, and expressed her intense grief and pathos after having cared for her mother during her illness. Her stream-of-consciousness expression of mourning, "Through Deep Waters," connects her to all those who have walked through the valley of the shadow of death with a beloved one.

"Love and death! The two saddest and yet the two sweetest words in the world. Love! The power [with] which one's being passes from the darkness of night into the glad light of morning. The passion which makes all earth sweet and beautiful; which makes all life joyous and seems to bring heaven nearer—yet so often fraught with pain, with sorrow, sometimes almost unbearable, yet precious because it is for love's sake . . . Mother—the one most like God this side of heaven; the personification of purity, patience and love.

They have laid her away and I am alone. Alone! . . Oh thou Great Helper! I cannot pray, I can only sob: Mother!"

Mabel loved her Methodist church in Dubuque and once wrote from India that "a pang of longing darted through my heart when I looked at the calendar you enclosed of dear St. Luke's . . . but the Lord is just as near here, rather nearer I think, and I would not exchange this consciousness of His presence for the finest church on earth." It was these Methodist women in Dubuque who paid $2 each month for Mabel's salary of $600 per year.

On learning at age ninety that her eyesight was failing, Mabel hurriedly read all of Shakespeare's plays within a two-week period so that she could reflect on them when her eyesight failed completely. Upper Iowa University, where Mabel had earned both bachelor's and master's degrees, honored her with a Doctor of Humanities degree.

While Mabel waited for Stanley in their supposed retirement home in Orlando, Florida, Stanley continued his ministry, and could not bring himself to retire rather than work. Stanley once said, "Mabel is the sweetest girl in the world," and admitted that she "fills up beautifully the 'lacks' in my nature—which are many." Mabel once told son-in-law Jim that she "would rather have E. Stanley Jones for two weeks a year than any other man for fifty-two!" A family friend spoke of Mabel as being "common, warm, friendly, loveable and so proud of her husband."

At the age of ninety-five Mabel fell and broke a hip. Eunice and Jim moved her closer to them, first to the United Methodist Country House in Wilmington, Delaware, and later even closer to Gaithersburg, Maryland. Mabel died peacefully on Friday, June 23, 1978, at the age of one hundred years, after a century of God-anointed global ministry.

Iowa inducted Mabel posthumously into the Women's Hall of Fame in Des Moines where Eunice received the reward on behalf of her mother on the day that commemorates the milestone in 1920 when women received the right to vote. While "women's work for women" gradually dwindled into disuse in mission work during this time, Mabel and others like her further obliterated the notion that a man's work is more important than a woman's work.

From the perspective of maturity when her mother died, Eunice described her as a "strict, though fair disciplinarian, a very private person, always resourceful and self-sufficient. Her faith was quiet and inward—appropriate to her Quaker background—rather than demonstrative, exceedingly reflective, with a great knack of thinking things through carefully before she acted. She was a gifted teacher, an able and aggressive administrator while not yielding one iota of femininity. Finally, she was a deeply committed Christian woman, a servant of God and of all the people. Somehow I know her service is acceptable to the One who inspired it."

Self-reliance, Eunice says, was her mother's greatest gift to her. Looking at Eunice's life and accomplishments, it is obvious that both Stanley and Mabel instilled in her a global vision, a pervasive core of independence and a commitment to India and its peoples. Mischievous humor wraps Eunice's forthrightness in gentility. Skill and ingenuity earmark her success as missionary and historian, writer and editor, parent and helpmeet, public speaker and fund-raiser—and not so incidentally, service to the United Methodist Church, the communities in which she lived, and her country.

* * * * *

Mabel likely did not realize the nearly incomprehensible honor of a relationship and correspondence with Mahatma Gandhi for twenty-five years, all on post cards, regarding education and

More than name-dropping, narratives of association with famous personages belong in Eunice's story. Her companion of nearly seventy years sums it up this way: "There is such a mingling of lives that even separate identity seems somewhat obscured. What one does, both do . . ."

"Eunice has been my most constant, stern, and usually constructive critic, often snatching me back at the very brink of what might have been disastrous decisions." Jim found that sometimes non-advice is the best wisdom.

Once when desperate for counsel, Jim attempted to reach Eunice by phone, but overseas communication was difficult, at best. Like Stanley, Jim had been elected a bishop in India, but he favored the election of an Indian national. After all, he reasoned, the Methodist church was (then) celebrating its hundred-year existence in India. Needing Eunice's advice and support, Jim finally reached her. She responded simply, as Ruth did to Naomi in Old Testament lore, "Where you go, I will go." But Jim did not accept.

discipline. Or, we might say that Gandhi, too, did not realize his privilege of a relationship with Mabel Jones!

One day when Stanley Jones was visiting Mahatma Gandhi, a letter and package arrived from Kamala Nehru, wife of Jawaharlal Nehru who was hospitalized in Switzerland for tuberculosis. Their daughter was Indira who married a Parsee named Gandhi. The Joneses as well as Eunice and Jim enjoyed a close friendship with her. In the package for the Mahatma, a letter from Kamala accompanied an exquisitely woven tea cloth: "I have spun the thread; I have woven the cloth and embroidered it for you."

Although Gandhi appreciated the gift, he had no use for it in his sparse lifestyle, so he gave it Stanley telling him, "Give it to Mrs. Jones with my love."

After her mother's death, Eunice found the cloth carefully preserved in its wrapping, accompanied by its history. Gently smoothing its folds and appreciating its value, she took a picture of it to show Prime Minister Indira Gandhi who remembered seeing her mother working on the exquisite piece. She had wondered what happened to it. Eunice intended to give it to her on her next visit, but before she could return to India, Prime Minister Gandhi had been assassinated. In characteristic generosity, Eunice determined to give it to her son, Rajiv Gandhi, who had then become prime minister himself. Rajiv was moved to tears as he fingered the cloth that his grandmother—whom he had never seen—had woven, that Gandhi had given to Mabel who had protected it, and that Eunice had passed on to him. It is now in the Indira Gandhi Museum in New Delhi.

The actors in this drama—Kamala, Indira, Mahatma and Rajiv, along with Stanley, Mabel, Jim and Eunice—all left their fingerprints on this tea cloth. In a larger sense, their fingerprints touch the whole world. But Mabel, with her typical frugality, and Eunice, through her customary generosity and thoughtfulness, provided denouement that will live on in both Methodist and Indian history for generations yet unborn.

Chapter 10

A Hero's Welcome

They change their sky, but not their souls
who cross the ocean.
—Latin poet Horace

After living ten years in Montclair, New Jersey, the trajectory for Eunice and Jim once again catapulted them—not away from India and global interests, but to an even more capacious worldview and ministry in the global village.

Although not a delegate in 1960 to the Northeastern Jurisdictional Conference, in his role as Associate General Secretary of Global Mission Jim met with a group there that planned to establish a university in the (then) Belgian Congo. As he was leaving for the airport to attend another meeting, a delegate asked Jim to stay longer in order to address the conference on a delicate matter that related to a bishop already serving in Africa. Jim's expertise in global perspective lent itself to speaking to the body for ten minutes, after which he rushed to the airport. Once again, Providence is at work!

When he finally returned home from his speaking engagements, his family greeted him with less than enthusiasm. Daughter Jan was crying and son Stan would not even speak to him. Who died? What happened? Thinking the worst, he asked weakly, "Whatever is wrong?" To his utter shock Eunice replied, "They've elected you bishop!" The Conference had not been able to reach Jim, so relayed the startling news to Eunice. They packed quickly to return to Washington, D.C., arriving at 3:00 a.m. That morning they were presented to the Conference and learned of Jim's assignment to the Boston area.

So it was that in 1960, Eunice prepared the children for another big move and another new life. While interviewing Jim, a reporter for the *Boston Globe* asked eight year-old Stan about New England. "Do you know where Maine is?" to which Stan replied. "I'm not quite sure, but I think it's somewhere off the coast of Kansas."

Once again Eunice turned from her cherished friends, lovely home and rose garden to create another home in Newtonville, Massachusetts. At the Christmas gathering Eunice shone her hospitality on the crowd of district superintendents gathered in

Before his election Jim had already been scheduled to preach at the National Cathedral in Washington, D. C., for the Thanksgiving service, but the tragic assassination of President Kennedy on November 22, 1963, led Jim to call from Boston to withdraw as preacher. They insisted that he keep the appointment that would be telecast instead as a national service of mourning. Jim spent the night preparing a new sermon entitled, "The Gift of a Man," and flew to Washington.

Engrossed in his manuscript even en route, he felt some anxiety. Jim's seatmate expressed interest in Jim's concentrated effort. When Jim asked if he wanted to read it, he perused it critically. He turned out to be an angel/writer/editor in disguise. Gore Vidal, author and half-brother of Jacqueline Kennedy, invited Jim to ride with him in the limousine that dropped Jim at his hotel.

their home. Jim's office in Boston was across the street from Trinity Episcopal Church where he had received his call to India in 1937. Not far away was Tremont Street Methodist Episcopal Church, where women first broke through male dominance to establish the Woman's Foreign Mission Society.

It was also in that eventful place that Mabel Lossing was commissioned and sent to India where she was destined to marry E. Stanley Jones. So, Jim and Eunice joyfully embraced the area to which Jim was assigned.

Eunice soon ingratiated herself into the community to which Jim was appointed, not only in a supportive role, but also as a social activist. During the late 1960s, Matthew P. Dumont, M.D., assistant commissioner for drug rehabilitation for Massachusetts, asked Eunice to write *Drug Abuse: Summons to Community Action* for The North Conway Institute that provided the Commonwealth a sense of purpose and direction in a critical and confused area. Dumont said that the Institute took a bold and creative step by commissioning "an intelligent, open-minded, sensitive and articulate [layperson] to find out what she could about the drug scene in Massachusetts and what is being done about it at the community level."

First published in the *Boston Globe*, fifty thousand of the books were next distributed to schools, churches, state agencies, federal armed forces agencies, libraries, hospitals, YMCAs, the St. Paul Council on Alcohol Problems and Drug Abuse, the Massachusetts Council of Churches and Boston's drug seminar, stretching along the east coast from New England to Florida.

In it, Eunice described six case histories of community response to drug issues that she recognized as symptomatic—"not so much of pathological children and families as [symptomatic] of complex and profound social issues . . . to single out the drug user either as 'sick' or 'criminal' is to make a serious mistake." Dumont wrote that while not de-emphasizing the dangers of widespread drug use, "Eunice Mathews manages to avoid the panic and rage that causes so many people to turn to hastily conceived panaceas or repressive police tactics as a way of controlling their anxiety."

In addition to the case studies, Eunice included classification and description of drugs and their effects. She discussed the origin of such drugs as marijuana, a common weed throughout India, the rest of Asia, Africa and the Western world. She also prepared a section on Drugs and the Law, and another on Penalties for Illegal Trade under U. S. Federal Law.

* * * * *

Among innumerable accomplishments during the years in which Jim—Bishop Mathews—served as an episcopal leader in the Methodist Church, he appointed Margaret Hendrickson of the Maine Conference as the first woman district superintendent in the United States. A collective gasp—and groans from some—followed the announcement. A woman? But the bishop's action is hardly surprising with a spouse and mother-in-law who long defied stereotypes.

In her own courageously conscientious way, Eunice once refuted information presented by a historian in a public meeting, leading to a prompt and unexpected vote for Eunice Mathews to be the vice-president of the General Commission on Archives and History (GCAH) for that quadrennium. Once again, in her mother's footsteps, Eunice became the first woman—and certainly the first wife of a bishop—to assume a position regarded as male domain. Serving with Bishop Scott Allen, chair of the body, she often presided in his absence, and strongly influenced Charles Yrigoyen's election as the General Secretary of GCAH, housed at Drew University in Madison, New Jersey.

Again, like her mother, Eunice's acceptance of "what is" facilitated the extraordinary contributions she and Jim accomplished together, both in the States and abroad. When Jim was a delegate to the World Council of Churches meeting in New Delhi in late 1961, Eunice was ready to return to India as well. Fortuitously, they also wanted the older two children to acquire fluency in a foreign language. So, leaving eight year-old son Stan with an uncle in Texas in exchange for his son, Eunice enrolled the three pre-teens in College Cevenol, a French Huguenot School in the Cevenne Mountains of southern France. Fluent French accompanied them home after a year in school there. And Eunice once again was able to visit her "homeland" of India.

Typical of a youngest sibling, however, Stan complained that unlike his older sisters, he never got to "go anywhere." Much to his surprise, Jim announced to Stan that he would accompany his dad on a trip around the world. On his return Stan wrote a school report expressing the value of the trip that introduced him to "the hate in Leopoldville, the refugees and the homeless in India and Hong Kong, and the good job missionaries are doing all over the world."

Stan would later graduate from Columbia with a Ph.D. in architecture and currently teaches at Hobart College in New York. His father describes him as "a gifted teacher, highly creative . . . possessing skill in combining theory and practice." Indeed, Stanley's prophetic statement as a twelve-year-old poet and writer he now fulfills through his teaching/art profession: " . . . [the trip] will help me in my later years, because you can't face the world until you know what the world is facing."

On another trip to India, Eunice and Jim met a lay evangelist who had advanced kidney disease. Given three months to live, he was brought to Houston, Texas, to await a kidney transplant, facilitated by the Mathewses and Bishop Ben Oliphint. Finally they got the word, the tragedy and the joy of it: A young man in Houston had been killed in an accident, and his kidney was a perfect match. Dhinakaran subsequently lived up to his name as "maker of daylight," preaching the Gospel to his people for years thereafter.

An extraordinary event propelled Eunice to Italy with Jim. Once again, for Eunice it was like going home. They counted as a high privilege to observe, and later to participate in, the modern miracle of Vatican II. Spectacular as a rose opening in spring, "the impossible had happened, the immobile had moved . . . a new openness characterized the Roman Church," Jim wrote from the perspective of one committed to the ecumenical movement.

Then in 1966, Pope Paul VI received Eunice and Jim at his summer residence in Castel Gondolfo. He gave Eunice a gold medallion of Saints Peter and Paul, and to Jim a commemorative silver piece recalling the Pope's visit to Bombay. He was most interested in the fact that Eunice and Jim's church was but a hundred yards from the image of the "Gateway to India" on the obverse of her medallion, and that she had been born in India of missionary parents. His parting words were: "Though we may not be one in this life, we shall be one in heaven."

At the re-opening of John Wesley's Chapel on City Road, London, Eunice and Jim met Queen Elizabeth II and Prince Philip. Then at Windsor Castle an ecclesiastical group gathered for an audience with the Queen during which she made this poignant remark, "Today no nation may conduct its affairs as if other nations did not exist."

On the home front, Eunice and Jim participated in another memorable occasion celebrated in Honolulu on the fiftieth anniversary of Japan's surrender. Asked to present President Clinton, Jim flew with Eunice on Air Force One with the Clintons, also flying part way on the back-up Boeing 707. It was on that plane that John F. Kennedy's body was carried to Washington and Lyndon Johnson was sworn in as president. At the service Jim spoke on behalf of veterans, living and dead, quoting President George H. W. Bush who said, referring to the Japanese, "We made our enemies our friends . . ." a goal that the Mathewses continue to espouse as the Christian high road.

Honored by having served on the committee that worked together to build the Interfaith Chapel at Camp David, Jim and Eunice sat with President and Mrs. George H.W. Bush at the barbecue they hosted following its dedication. The United Methodist contractor K. H. Plummer built much of Camp David. Artist/designer Dr. Rudolph Sandon, a European immigrant, presented the stained glass windows as an expression of gratitude to his adoptive land. Each window depicts symbols from the major faiths.

Eunice counts as an especially high moment the event following Martin Luther King's election for the Nobel Peace Prize. Both King and E. Stanley Jones had been nominated for the honor. While waiting in line to congratulate him, Eunice was stopped by King who told her that he wanted to speak with her. He explained that it was her father's book, *Gandhi: Portrayal of a Friend*, that clarified and mobilized his understanding of non-violent resistance. Today in Martin Luther King's museum in Atlanta, a book on a stand lies open to a page written by Jones about his friend Gandhi. Printed by Martin Luther King across a page that describes non-violent resistance—not as passive, but intensely active—are these words: THIS IS IT! King had found the springboard into his Dream that led to the revolution of Civil Rights in the United States.

* * * * *

In 1972 Jim and Eunice had moved to face new opportunities in the Washington/Baltimore area that included two conferences. As no episcopal residence was provided, they bought their first home, where they lived until moving into an apartment in the year 2000. On numerous occasions, Eunice served as Jim's secretary. Altogether during his episcopacy, including interim appointments after retirement, he served ten annual conferences—all a part of Eunice's experience, as well.

Having been born in India, Eunice was an American citizen with no hometown. So Baltimore Mayor Schaefer during their time in the Washington/Baltimore Area, honored Eunice by making her a citizen of Baltimore, Maryland, the hometown of her father, E. Stanley Jones.

Eunice could not have imagined that her early training in secretarial skills following college graduation would be the backbone throughout her own ministry, beginning as her father's assistant. Following his stroke, Eunice's father had continued to use an electronic recorder—"with too many buttons." By placing a piece of tape over the "delete" button, Eunice preserved much of his dictation for his last book that she prepared for publication. She typed and edited twenty-five published books by her father, E. Stanley Jones. Without her skill and ability to organize and edit, not to mention read both her father's and her husband's scrawl referred to by some as penmanship, their publications may never have reached the world.

When Bishop Mathews' memoirs were published in 2000, he credited Eunice with deciphering his handwriting, "seeing it through many revisions . . . serving as constructive critic and constant companion." He suggested his memoirs should be entitled: "We Did It Together."

"Our stories have been so tightly melded together," Jim praises Eunice with these words, "that our separate experiences are hard to distinguish. [Eunice] has proved understanding of the heavy demands that have been put upon me. She has tried to relieve many of the pressures to which I was subjected and has all too often shielded me from stresses by taking them upon herself."

Yet, she fulfilled her own mission in many areas, such as presenting a history of United Methodist Women to Metropolitan Memorial UMW in Washington, D.C. This impressive document, printed in 1989, is titled *Recollections on Our Heritage as United Methodist Women*. Remarkable, not only in content, but also in its scope, she showcases women as change-agents, holding hands around the globe, as richly pervasive and undeniably vital as a network of capillaries.

In it, Eunice referred to the adage familiar to Methodists in earlier centuries, "organizing to beat the devil." She wrote about the "Methodist genius for seizing upon a good cause to support, or some social evil to combat and then proposing an organization to do so." She built on the examples of devoted women like Mary the mother of Jesus and Dorcas, ancient forerunners of Susannah Wesley and Barbara Heck, followed by such giants as Isabella

Thoburn in India, whose statue stands over one of the arches in the Washington National Cathedral, and Mrs. H. D. McGavock, who secretly gave diamonds from her wedding veil, valued at a thousand dollars, to build Glopton School in Shanghai.

She wrote about the Evangelical United Brethren woman who established a refuge for girls being sold into child marriage in Sierra Leone, and the tragedy there in 1898 of an uprising in which all the missionaries but one were slaughtered. She did not forget the advent of the Methodist Deaconess movement, initiated in India, that provided social service centers, including the Traveler's Aid Society that one still finds at airports even today.

Eunice recalled stories of Mary McLeod Bethune, daughter of slaves, who built her school—now Bethune Cookman College—on a dump in Daytona, Florida; she wrote of Belle Harris Bennett, who accepted no salary for her work with Cubans, African Americans and Mexicans, and founded what is now Scarritt College in Nashville, and established work in Kentucky, China, Africa, Japan and Brazil, where Bennett College is found in Rio de Janeiro.

Not forgotten was the woman missionary in Malaya who once received a letter addressed merely thus: M.M.; M.G.H.S; K.L. (Mabel Marsh; Malaya Girls High School; Kuala Lumpur)! Eunice also wrote of educators such as her own mother Mabel Lossing Jones (India), Jennie Chapin (Argentina), Dora Schoonmaker (Japan), Mary Sharpe (Liberia), Layona Glenn (Brazil), Flemmie Kitrall (from Howard University to University of Baroda), Amanda Smith ("black saint" and global evangelist), Georgia Harkness (Japan) and Clara Swain, who established the first hospital for women in Asia.

Women such as Harriet Stubbs (Wyandots) worked with Native Americans from Alaska (Aleuts) to North Carolina (Cherokee) and others, adding more Native Americans than any other Protestant denomination to Christianity. Eunice highlighted scores of Methodist women other than Americans who became leaders in their countries, such as Rebecca Donoso (Chile), Ivy Chou

(Sarawak), Sarah Chako (India, who became a president of the World Council of Churches), Joyce Singa (Zimbabwe), and Helen Kim, who built the largest Methodist university for women in the world in Korea.

The works of these dedicated women and countless others—literally—at home in the global village comprise a litany of praise to God. They would not count their losses as sacrifices, but rather embrace the One who sent them into the world to serve, as expressed in this hymn by E. Margaret Clarkson:

"So send I you, my strength to know in weakness,
My joy in grief, my perfect peace in pain,
To prove my pow'r, my grace, my promised presence,
So send I you, eternal fruit to gain."

* * * * *

Eunice as servant continues to embody the spirit of radical hospitality and gracious giving that characterized her childhood gift of her Effanbee doll to her young friend, the child bride and mother at the age of thirteen. She admits that now, when people surreptitiously question her about her inheritance from her parents, she tells them that her father left her one thousand dollars—true, but what they may fail to understand is the legacy of immeasurable value.

Indeed, Eunice received far more than one grand in the mandate her father gave on his deathbed in Bareilly at the Clara Swain Hospital: He requested that his only offspring, with her husband, would manage the funds to ensure that these missional works in India would continue to flourish: the Mabel Jones Boys School (so named in 1961), the ***Nur Manzil*** Psychiatric Center (founded by E. Stanley Jones), the United Christian Ashrams worldwide (an outgrowth of E. Stanley Jones' Sat Tal ashram), and scholarships for schools and deserving individuals.

A look at these institutions is convincing enough. The Mabel Jones Boys School continues to educate and shape young lives to this day. When Mabel was sent to "rescue" the school, little did anyone expect that by her sheer work, will and faith she would change elementary education for boys throughout north India. Through her courageous innovations, not only are women teachers acceptable for boys, but a new respect for women pervades the system and the lives of now grown men who benefited from her tutelage. Even today, about a thousand boys continue to be educated each year through Mabel's scholarships.

Then, in addition to the ecumenical ashram movement that Stanley established, he also initiated in Lucknow the first institution for family psychiatry in India. Aptly named Nur Manzil Psychiatric Center, meaning Palace of Light, it provides services especially for the indigent, including children, to whom psychiatric services were previously unavailable. Continuing to function today, it is funded in part by the Mathews' establishment of an endowment to benefit the poor.

Also, the first women's hospital in Asia, founded by Dr. Clara Swain, is a miraculous monument to answered prayers of Swain and the wife of the first Methodist missionary to India. The Butlers were among the few missionaries to survive the ***Sepoy Rebellion*** in 1857. William Butler had written home that "all is lost, save life and the grace of God . . . Shall we give up because heaven and hell have risen up against us? Nay. Greater is he that is for us than all that can be against us!"

When William's wife, Clementina Rowe Butler, saw women lying along the shore of the Ganges River, their heads resting on the banks of the river with their feet in the water, she learned that they awaited death's deliverance. Neither treatment nor food was offered to the poor. When they mercifully died, a male relative pushed the body into the "sacred waters [that] would assure it the blessing of salvation."

On seeing this, both Swain and Butler determined to establish a hospital for women—long the largest women's hospital in Asia—whose religion did not allow a male doctor to touch them. In Bareilly, where Dr. Swain had been treating women in makeshift quarters, their vision ignited when Swain noticed an estate of forty-two acres with a dilapidated mansion, owned by the ***Nawab***. She contacted officials with her request for one acre. "Impossible!" spat the spokesperson. "The Nawab hates Christians." Swain's incessant prayers and persistence finally got her an audience with the raj who refused to listen to her well-prepared speech for long. He raised his hand dismissively, like a physical blow to Clara's face and certainly to her spirits.

But he then said, "I give it to you. Here, take it, take it! I give it to you with pleasure for this noble purpose"—not one acre, but the whole forty-two acres with mansion, dilapidated or not!

It was in this oldest hospital in Bareilly, India, that E. Stanley Jones would breathe his last breath. Having suffered a brain stem stroke in the States, he underwent rehabilitation in Boston, but begged to return to India. Jim, along with Stan and Anne, took Stanley back to the land he loved and taught him to walk again. But he contracted pneumonia and died peacefully there in January 1973.

Missionary Mabel Wagner acknowledged in a letter to Mabel after his death that Mabel had a unique share of grace to have given "Uncle Stanley" the freedom to follow the way he chose, but his "faith in Christ as Lord of both hurts and happiness has blessed us," said Wagner, "and we thank God for him and for you."

It was here, five years later, that Mabel joined Stanley in the Bishop's Lot at Mt. Olivet Cemetery in Baltimore, Maryland, where Bishop Francis Asbury is also interred. A Methodist time-capsule buried there is to be opened in 2066.

Clearly, Eunice's legacy mandated a lifetime of involvement in the work her parents had established. Such an "inheritance" is hardly typical, but she embraces the gift as it continues to grow exponentially along with her devotion and love for the Indian people, her parents and her God. Where her heart is, there is her treasure.

Eunice tells about the frantic letters from her girlhood Indian friend Mary Thomas Badhwar, who became a physician and married a remarkable man. Aware that she was dying of lung cancer, Mary begged Eunice to leave as soon as possible on an anticipated visit to India. "We must talk! Hurry!" she told Eunice. Her beloved husband Billy had died, and she needed to make her will. During her visit, Eunice reminded her friend of some facts about her heritage as a Methodist and her early interest in the Nur Manzil Hospital in her home town of Lucknow.

Hearing nothing further in the weeks after Mary's death, Eunice wondered whether her childhood friend had left anything to continue her parents' work. Mary did indeed—one and a quarter million dollars to Nur Manzil Psychiatric Hospital, and the same amount to help support the children and widows of Indian preachers.

Eunice continues to challenge the Mission Support Network (MSN) of bishops' spouses to raise funds in her gentle yet persuasive way. "I hate to play the beggar's role," she said in one more presentation, "but am willing to do so again in order to keep faith with the past." To keep faith with the past! Having already touched thousands throughout the world through her speaking, writing, fund-raising, living the Gospel—Eunice keeps on investing in the Indian people she loves.

In 2004 the General Secretary of the General Board of Global Mission presented Eunice on her ninetieth birthday to the General Conference in Pittsburgh. In response she said, "I need not be defined by being the daughter of a renowned evangelist, nor as the wife of a bishop. I am free to be myself . . . a freedom I have in Jesus Christ!"

Although receiving a standing ovation, she understands herself to be the woman in the background. She ever lives the supporting role that would win an Oscar, were it cinema; her role is central to the plot. As Bishop Earl Hunt wrote, "One can never assess the varied and substantial accomplishments of [Bishop] Jim Mathews in either the missionary or the episcopal eras of his life without acknowledging the far more than usual role played in it all by his brilliant and extraordinary wife, Eunice Jones Mathews."

Although the New York cab driver didn't know Mabel Jones, nor did he even really know Eunice Jones Mathews, he had it right when he saw her. He knew a hero when he met one. These women epitomize the untold other half of the Methodist mission story—heroes indeed.

The familiar tale of the old missionary couple who returned by ship to the homeland following a lifetime of service overseas illustrates their story. Flags waved, cheers erupted, fireworks exploded, bands played. The old couple was overcome with emotion at the accolades—but it was not for them.

Realizing their mistake, they paused to watch the returning soldiers behind them marching down the gangplank, waving and shouting responses to the frenzied crowds. The old couple stepped aside to watch as they passed by. Before trudging down the walkway arm in arm, the shop-worn missionary whispered to his wife, "It's all right, dear; we're not home yet."

Epilogue

The past is not dead. It is not even past.
—William Faulkner

With her heart still in India, Eunice journeyed back to Sitapur. Setting out from his village, the old Muslim cook Bhulan began his own journey, a dust-choked half-day walk to the Methodist mission. Walking slowly in sync with his worn-out heart, he rehearsed the news:

"The Memsahib from America is coming to visit."

"Memsahib Mabel?"

"No, no, it is Baba Eunice. She is grown up now. You remember her . . ."

Of course he remembered.

"I must go," he announced.

As he walked he recalled having waited with the other servants who had gathered for the vigil. From the cookhouse he heard nothing, but he wanted to hear the baby's first cry. He moved closer to the big house and the other servants, praying for good news.

At last baba Eunice arrived. He smiled at memories of carrying her about, teaching her many words by pointing to objects and smiling at her efforts to talk. He pictured her grabbing just one more bite before Memsahib caught him feeding her hot curries that the child clearly enjoyed. He chuckled with glee at the memory of her sitting in her reading tree, or teaching her monkey to do tricks, or hugging her rabbit, or giggling at pranks she devised to startle wary visitors, or weeping as her mongoose Rikki was pulled from around her neck to be given away . . .

Quickening his steps in anticipation—although eighty-plus years makes a difference in a gait—after many hours he gazed beyond the neem trees at the mission bungalow nestled in an overgrowth of bougainvillea. At last he saw her. Grown up now, Eunice hurried down the sun-splashed path to greet him.

"Bhulan!" she cried, running toward him, arms spread wide. Her best friend and confidante of childhood suddenly paused, looking so stooped, so old, his skin stretched like crinkled brown parchment over his thin cheeks. Squinting, he waited for her approach, then lifted his arms to receive her.

She'd almost forgotten that he cared so much, and felt again the surge of love that wrapped them in its warmth. Time stood still. They clung to each other, to the memory of their shared history, to the joy of their mutual love.

Their journey will never end. It will continue beyond the miles and cultures, the religions and years that separate them for this brief interlude in the Sea of God's eternity . . .

* * * * *

The last time I saw Eunice and Jim together, I watched from a distance as Eunice walked with her husband, stooped and faltering as he continued recovery from a stroke, to a table where other bishops were seated. Then she quietly sat down with the spouses of bishops. There were no great crowds, no stirring accolades, no clapping or cheering for this extraordinary couple. I forced myself to take a seat rather than announce to the crowd with a bullhorn: "Everyone please rise to give a hero's welcome to Jim and Eunice Jones Mathews!"

But I did not do so. Swallowing hard, I reminded myself of this: They aren't home yet.

A Taste of India

MULLIGATAWNEY SOUP

This is Eunice Mathews' modified version of a South India dish that the British found difficult to pronounce. Too tasty to ignore, they re-named it to suit their taste. The rice she serves with it is basmati, a Hindi word meaning "fragrant," grown in the foothills of the Himalayas.

2 lbs. chicken (1 package each of breast quarters and thigh quarters do well)
2 or 3 large onions, sliced
whole spices:
  1 or 2 sticks cinnamon
  6 whole cloves
  2 or 3 bay leaves
salt
1 can coconut milk (or, ½ pint whole milk)
2 ounces desiccated coconut (non-sweet)
2 Tablespoons cooking oil or olive oil
½ of a 6-ounce can tomato puree
ground spices:
  2 teaspoons turmeric
  ½ teaspoon cloves
  ½ teaspoon cinnamon
  2 teaspoons cumin
  3 teaspoons coriander
  1 teaspoon cardamom
  2 teaspoons black pepper
ground almonds
gram flour
lemons

Remove chicken skin/fat. Cut into small pieces. Cover with water. Add whole spices and salt to taste. Add onion, but reserve one for later step. Cover and bring to boil; simmer until cooked. Strain. Keep stock. Remove cooked onions to mash—then add to soup later. Separate meat from bones.

In smaller pan: Bring to boil the coconut milk and coconut. Simmer until liquid is reduced to just over half; add more milk, or water, if liquid is reduced too much.

Fry one onion in large pan until golden brown. Add ground spices and tomato puree. Stir while cooking on low heat until blended. Add stock and meat and mashed onions. Bring to boil. Remove from heat. Season with salt. Add coconut milk mixture and ground almonds. Thicken with gram flour. Heat—but do not boil.

Serve with rice and lemon slices.

NAAN

This is the most common of the North India breads, traditionally cooked on the walls of a very hot tandoor (clay oven). If you have a baking stone, all the better, but otherwise, grease a pizza pan or baking sheet. Preheat oven to 500° F.

2 tablespoons very warm—but not hot—water
1 package quick-acting yeast
1 teaspoon white sugar
½ teaspoon baking powder
½ teaspoon salt
2½–3 cups plain flour
¾ cup thick plain yogurt
4 tablespoons melted butter
1 egg, beaten

Preheat oven to 500 degrees. Stir together first three ingredients in a small dish or measuring cup. Wait about ten minutes until it foams. Meanwhile, measure 2½ cups flour with salt and baking powder into a bowl and make a well in center. Add yogurt, melted butter and beaten egg into the well with the yeast mixture. Mix well and add more flour as needed to knead into a smooth ball, no longer sticky. Add a little oil to hands and knead dough for 5–8 minutes until smooth and satiny. Cover with lightly damp cloth and let rise in a warm place until double in bulk, about 1½–2 hours.

Divide the dough into eight pieces and flatten into pear shapes. Place 2–3 on a greased baking sheet or stone, and bake on top shelf for 3 minutes; they will puff up and slightly brown. Brush tops with melted butter.

CARROT HALWA

This simple sweet dessert looks best when bright orange carrots are used, but tastes delicious even with the eyes closed. This is definitely an Americanized adaptation of this sweet, simple dessert.

4 cups grated carrots
2 cups milk
4 tablespoons ghee* or melted butter
1 cup white sugar (or use Splenda)
½ cup golden raisins
½ cup brown raisins
½ teaspoon cardamom
½ cup slivered almonds
½ cup pistachios
ground cardamom

Slowly simmer the grated carrots in the milk over low heat until the carrots are tender and the milk evaporates. Be careful not to scorch/burn the mixture by keeping it on low heat and stirring often. Add the ghee (or butter) and cook until the carrots begin to brown.

Add the sugar and continue cooking on low until the mixture is thick and dry. Add raisins, cardamom and almonds. Serve warm in small bowls with cream or whipped cream, sprinkled with a little cardamom. Garnish with extra slivered almonds/crushed pistachios.

*Ghee is clarified butter, made by melting butter until the whey separates from the curd. Pour off the liquid and save the fat, known as ghee or ghi.

MANGO LASSI

The lassi is a popular drink with Indian foods and easy to prepare.

1 large ripe mango
1 cup cold whole milk
1 cup plain thick yogurt

Chop or process the mango and add a pinch of salt. Push through a sieve with the back of a spoon. Discard the fibers. Blend mango with the milk and yogurt, either by hand or in a blender. You could serve as is, or blend with 6–8 ice cubes until it is a thick, creamy, cold smoothie.

Glossary

Allah—The name of God in Islam.

Amrit Bazar Patrika—Newspaper in Calcutta (Kolkata).

anna—one-sixteenth of a rupee, the Indian monetary exchange, although India now uses the decimal system.

ashram—A religious community that meets to pray and study, common among Indians, but also Christian ashrams have spread globally, initiated by E. Stanley Jones.

atta—A whole-wheat dough used in making chappattis.

ayah—An Indian nanny, sometimes a maid to the lady of the house.

baba—A child, a baby.

Babu—A courtesy title in Hindi.

banyan tree—Common in India, it throws down shoots from its branches to root in the ground, sometimes forming an enormous display of "trunks."

Bhagavad-Gita—The sacred Hindu text of Sanskrit text, in which Krishna reveals himself as the Supreme Being.

bhisti—The water carrier who drew water and delivered it.

Birla House—The home of the wealthy industrialist Birla, and Gandhi's "home" in New Dehli, where he died after being shot.

Bombay—The most populous city of India and the capital of Maharashtra State, the name has evolved through the centuries and is currently called Mumbai.

boxwalla—Those of the merchant/tradesman class.

Brahmin—The highest caste in the Hindu caste system; educated Indians such as priests, scholars and teachers are included in this caste.

burra din—"A great day" in the Hindi language.

Calcutta—Now called Kolkata, on the east bank of the River Hooghly, it is the capital of the Indian state of West Bengal in eastern India. Formerly the capital of India during British rule, it is the second largest city after Mumbai.

cardamom—a tropical plant, the seeds and pods of which are crushed to use as a spice.

charkha—The spinning wheel that became a national symbol in India.

coolie—A low-caste servant employed to do menial tasks.

Dalits—Another name for the "untouchables" of the Hindu caste system who perform the lowliest tasks, such as collecting human waste from homes, sweeping the streets, picking up dead bodies, hauling water in pigskin bags—utter defilement.

dandy—A box-like conveyance carried by four people, used in the mountains.

dhobi—The washerman.

Diwali—The Hindu Festival of Lights with Lakshimi, the goddess of wealth, presiding when the new year begins.

dowry—The practice in which the bride's family gives the groom goods and/or money. In reverse dowry, the groom pays the bride's family for a valuable wife.

Gandhiji—The suffix refers to one greatly beloved, often used for Mohandas Gandhi.

ghats—The place where Hindus burn their dead.

gram flour—made from chick peas

griot—The African person who memorizes the stories of the people and passes them on orally to the next generation.

gulab jamins—Sweet dessert shaped into small balls and fried like a donut, then dipped into warm sugar syrup.

harijans—Mahatma Gandhi coined this term, referring to the Hindu "untouchables" as "children of God."

Havabagh—Fresh air.

Himalayas—A Sanskrit word meaning "abode of snow," the mountains stretch through India, Nepal, Bhutan and Tibet; it has the ten highest peaks on earth, including Mt. Everest.

Hindi—The official language of India.

Hindu—An adherent of Hinduism, the dominant cultic religion of India.

Hindustani—A spoken rather than written dialect in northern India, comprised of Urdu and Hindi.

Humayun's tomb—An ancient mausoleum that was used to shelter refugees following the horrors after Independence in 1947.

jalabis—an Indian sweet dessert.

Jamkhed—A Methodist mission/hospital/village in Maharashtra State.

kabadhi—An Indian game played with two teams, involving intense self-defense, attack and counter-attack, now played world-wide.

kacha—Houses made from mud, thatch or other low-quality material, while pucca houses are made from high quality materials that can better withstand flooding.

Kali—The Hindu goddess of destruction and death.

karait—A common, small venomous snake in India.

Kashmir—Disputed territory shares borders with India, Pakistan, Afghanistan and China.

khadi—Homespun cotton.

Kshatriyas—The second caste of Hinduism, which includes the warriors.

Kumbh festival—The largest festival in the world, a legend birthed the celebration in the 7th century, and it continues annually in one of four Indian sites. More than 20 million gathered in 1992 for the social and religious event that has become known globally.

kurta-pyjama—A typical Indian man's fashion with an over-the-knee, loose fitting top and a pajama-like bottom.

Lal Bagh—Ruby Garden.

Lucknow—the capital city of Uttar Pradesh, the most populous state in India.

Mahatma—Great Soul, a title of deep respect for virtue and wisdom, often referring to Mohandas Gandhi.

Mahatma Gandhi ki jai—Victory to Mahatma Gandhi.

memsahib—A respectful address for the woman of the house.

Muslim—One who practices Islam, a monotheistic religion. Its holy book is the *Qur'an*. Some call its adherents Mohammedans, an inaccurate description, as they do not worship Mohammad, but Allah (God). They are also referred to as Moslems.

Mussoorie—A popular hill station in the Himalayas of North India and the site of the International School of Woodstock in the higher elevation of Landour, originally used for convalescing soldiers.

Naini Tal—A popular hill-station resort in the Kumaon Hills of the Himalayas where the Methodist Girls School, Wellesley, was located—now closed.

nawar—Rough, wide tape woven onto bed frames to support a mattress, often made of the fluffed covering of the seeds of the ceiba tree.

nawab—A Muslim leader of importance.

neem tree—Common in India, with medicinal value, its bark exudes a sticky tonic, the leaves and fruit an aromatic oil. Some use it to clean the teeth.

Nur Manzil—Meaning "Palace of Light," it is a family psychiatric care facility, especially for the indigent, established by E. Stanley Jones in Lucknow.

palaquin—A flat conveyance carried by four men.

pandal—A tent-like canopy.

Parsee—Zoroastrians of Persia, having descended from Persian refugees in 7th century.

Punjabi—The language and people of Punjab, between modern-day Pakistan and India.

punkah—Variously constructed fans, such as a board attached to canvas, moved by a coolie to circulate air.

purdah—The separation of Hindu and Muslim women from society by worn coverings or curtains.

Quit India—A term of Gandhi's that became the mantra for all of India, referring to ending British colonial rule, eventually embraced even by the British.

Qur'an or **Koran**—The sacred text of Islam.

raj or **rajah**—A ruler.

Ramadan—The Muslim month of fasting and prayer.

sahib—A respectful address for the man of the house.

Sanskrit—The extinct Indo-European language of ancient India.

sari—A long rectangular cloth worn wrapped and pleated around the waist and draped over the shoulder, typical garb of women of India.

Sat Tal—Location of the Christian ashram in India established by E. Stanley Jones and given to the Methodists. It means "Seven Lakes," of which four have dried up.

satyagraha—Truth-force. Acceptance of suffering, but never inflicting it on others.

Sepoy Rebellion—Referred to as the First War of Independence (1857), a mutiny of the native troops known as sepoys (who outnumbered the British army troops ten to one), resulting in widespread bloodshed, with the British eventually regaining control.

Sevagran—Location of Gandhi's home and ashram.

shikari—A small paddleboat included with a houseboat in Kashmir for side excursions.

Shudras—The fourth caste in the Hindu caste system that includes servants/workers who serve the upper class.

Sikh—A religious group, an offshoot of Hinduism, known as "people of the Book."

Sitapur—A town in Uttar Pradesh state in north India, north-northwest of Lucknow, where the Methodist Mabel Jones Boys School is located.

suttee—The Hindu practice of a widow's burning to death by throwing herself on the pyre of her deceased husband rather than be relegated to lifetime banishment/ostracism.

swaraj—Home rule.

Taj Mahal—A magnificent monument to the favorite wife, Mumtaz Mahal, of Mughal Emperor Shah Jahan, completed in the seventeenth century in Agra.

Urdu—The official language of Pakistan, parts of North India and Bangladesh where Muslims are strong.

Vaishyas—The third caste of the Hindu caste system, which includes merchants and landowners.

wallahs—Merchants or tradesmen.

zenana—A part of the house for women and girls beginning at puberty.

SOURCES CITED

Adams, Lucy Neely. *52 Hymn Story Devotions*. Nashville: Abingdon Press, 2000.

Bumiller, Elizabeth. *May You Be the Mother of a Thousand Sons*. New York: Fawcett Columbine, 1990.

Chamberlain, Martha and Mary B. Adams. *Hymn Devotions for All Seasons*. Nashville: Abingdon Press, 1989.

Dear, John. *Mohandas Gandhi: Essential Writings*. Maryknoll, New York: Orbis Books, 2002.

Dough, Whitney J. *Sayings of E. Stanley Jones*. Franklin, Tennessee: Providence House Publishers, 1994.

Editors of Time-Life Books. *What Life Was Like in the Jewel of the Crown, British India 1600–1905*. Alexandria, Virginia, 1999.

Forster, E. M. *A Passage to India*. San Diego: Harcourt Brace Jovanovich, Inc., 1924.

General Board of Global Ministries, Women's Division. *They Went Out Not Knowing: 100 Women in Mission*. New York: GBGM, 1986.

Hendershot, Kathryn Reese. *E. Stanley Jones Had a Wife: The Life and Mission of Mabel Lossing Jones*. Lanham, Maryland, The Scarecrow Press and The Center for the Study of World Christian Revitalization Movements, 2007.

Jones, E. Stanley. *The Christ of the Indian Road*. Lucknow, India: Lucknow Publishing House, 1925, 1977.

Jones, E. Stanley. *Gandhi, Portrayal of a Friend*. Nashville: Abingdon Press, 1948.

Kaye, M. M. *The Far Pavillions*. New York: St. Martin's Press, 1997.

Mander, Harsh. *Unheard Voices: stories of forgotten lives*. New Delhi: Penguin Books India, 2001.

Mathews, Eunice Jones. *Drug Abuse: Summons to Community Action*. Boston: North Conway Institute, 1970.

Mathews, James K. *A Global Odyssey*. Nashville: Abingdon Press, 2000.

Mathews, James K. *The Matchless Weapon: Satyagraha*. Mumbai: Bharatiya Vidya Bhavan, 1989, 2004.

McPhee, Arthur J. *The Road to Delhi: Bishop Pickett Remembered, 1890–1981*. Bangalore, India: Saiacs Press, 2005.

Miller, J., A Kenedi, M. Wolfe. *Inside Islam: The Faith, the People and the Conflicts of the World's Fastest Growing Religion*. "Islam," Huston Smith, 11–26. New York: Marlowe, 2002.

Olson, James S. and Robert Shadle, eds. *Historical Dictionary of the British Empire, v.2*. Westport, Connecticut: Greenwood Press, 1996.

Philip, P.P. *A Survey of the Background, Origin and Growth of the Maramon Convention*. Tiruvalla: The T.A. M. Press, 1976.

Royis, Arundhati. *The God of Small Things*. New York: Harper Collins, 1998.

Scott, Paul. *The Raj Quartet: The Jewel in the Crown* (1966); *The Day of the Scorpion* (1968); *The Towers of Silence* (1971); *A Division of Spoils* (1975). Chicago: The University of Chicago Press, 1965-1975.

Sen, Amaryta. *The Argumentative Indian, Writings on Indian History, Culture and Identity*. New York: Farrar Giroux, 2005.

Suri, Manil. *The Death of Vishnu*. New York: W. W. Norton & Company, 2001.

The United Methodist Publishing House. "Lead, Kindly Light," *The United Methodist Hymnal*. Nashville: The United Methodist Publishing House, 1964, 1966.

The United Methodist Publishing House. "It Is Well with My Soul," *The United Methodist Hymnal*. Nashville: The United Methodist Publishing House, 1989, 2000.

Wickramasinghe, Priya and Carol Selva Rajah. *The Food of India*. London: Murdoch Books, 2002.

Wilson, Dorothy. *Palace of Healing*. New York: McGraw-Hill Book Company, 1968.

ARTICLES/REPORTS/SPEECHES/LYRICS

Alex Perry, "Bombay's Boom," *Time*, 26 June 2006, 40–43.

Aravind Adiga, "My Lost World," *Time*, 26 June 2006, 44–45.

Martha Chamberlain, "Ignore or Act." (Report prepared for the Mission Support Network and GBGM following observation/ training in Comprehensive Community-Based Health Care in urban Mumbai and rural Jamkhed, Maharashtra, India), 2001.

E. Margaret Clarkson, "So Send I You," *Singspiration Music*, Benson Music Group, 1964. Gospel hymn retrieved from: www.speroforum.com/site/print.asp?idarticle-=3656

Emily Wax, "Hindu Nationalists Win Key Vote in India," *The Washington Post*, A-9, 24 December 2007.

Emily Wax, "Female President Elected in India," *The Washington Post*, 22 July 2007.

Eunice and James K. Mathews, Christmas letters to friends, 2004–2006.

Eunice Jones Mathews, Her notes about childhood pets in India.

Eunice Jones Mathews, "Recollections on Our Heritage as United Methodist Women." Address given to the Metropolitan Memorial United Methodist Women, Washington, D.C., May 9, 1989.

Eunice Jones Mathews, "Christmas in India." Speech written for Metropolitan Memorial UMW, 2005.

Eunice Jones Mathews, Speech presented at luncheon of United Methodist Women in the Metropolitan United Methodist Church, Washington, D.C., 2007.

Evangeline Anderson-Rajkumar, "Restoring Dignity: Dalit Theology." *Response*, May 2005.

Megha Bahre, "Child Labor," *Forbes*, 25 February 2008, 72-29.

Michael Elliott, "India Awakens," *Time*, 26 June 2006, 36–39.

Paul Jeffrey, "Bible Women Spread Gospel, Empowerment," *Response*, May 2005, 24–27.

Paul Jeffrey, "Confronting Globalization," *Response*, May 2005, 16–21.

Paul Jeffrey, "Getting Credit and Respect," *Response*, May 2005, 20–21.

Paul Jeffrey, "Women at Risk: Gender Violence in India," *Response*, May 2005, 32–37.

Sally Howard, "Bhopal a Legacy of Indifference," *Response*, May 2006, 28–31.

Shashi Tharoor, "The Jewel in the Crown," *The Washington Post*, 26 March 2006. A review of *The Ruling Caste*, David Gilmore, New York: Farrar Giroux, 2006.

Shashi Tharoor, "A Passage to India," *The Washington Post*, 16 October 2005.

Viny Lal, "Jolly Good Fellows and Their Nasty Ways," *Times of India* (15 January 2007). A review of *The Blood Never Dried: A People's History of the British Empire*, John Newsinger. London: Bookmarks, 2006.

Viny Lal. Manus: Indian History and Politics. (Paper on history of British India). UCLA. Retrieved from [www.sscnet.ucla.edu/southasia/History/British/Brindia.html].

Wikipedia, Retrieved 2006 from [en.wikipedia.org/wiki/Indian_Rebellion_of_1857] "The Devil's Mind," Aftermath (6.1), *Company Rule in India*.

William Green, "How to Ride an Elephant," *Time*, June 26, 2006.

FILMS/DVDs

Earth, directed by Deepa Mehta, 1999. (One of a trilogy including *Fire* and *Water*.)

The Far Pavillions, directed by Peter Duffell, 1984.

Fire, directed by Deepa Mehta, 1997.

Gandhi, directed by Richard Attenborough, 1982.

A Jewel in the Crown, directed by Christopher Morahan and Jim O'Brien, 1985.

Monsoon Wedding, directed by Mira Nair, 2001.

A Passage to India, directed by David Lean, 1984.

Slumdog Millionaire, directed by Danny Boyle and Loveleen Tandan.

Water, directed by Deepa Mehta, 1985.

OTHER SOURCES

Numerous interviews and time spent with Eunice Jones Mathews, beginning in June, 2004. Visits, phone conversations and Internet communication continue.

Writings of Mabel Lossing Jones.

Interviews with Bishop James K. Mathews and Bishop Susan Morrison.

The United Methodist General Commission of Archives and History, located at Drew University in Madison, New Jersey, generously assisted by the General Secretary of GCAH, Robert J. Williams.

The staff at Handley Library, as well as the staff of Alson H. Smith Library at Shenandoah University, both in Winchester, Virginia.

About The Author

Eunice Mathews with Martha Chamberlain, October 2008

Born in Allentown, Pennsylvania, to a clergy father and English teacher mother, Martha Gunsalus Chamberlain graduated from United Wesleyan College, Sacred Heart Hospital School of Nursing and George Mason University. The United Methodist University of Liberia awarded her the Doctor of Humanities degree in 2004.

Married to Ray W. Chamberlain, Jr., ordained clergy, in 1960, she served four years in Zambia, Africa, as a missionary nurse, worked in psychiatric nursing and home health care and participated in a variety of missions. Especially meaningful was her visit to India to study comprehensive community-based primary healthcare (CCPH), focused on the needs of women and children. While there, she lost her heart to the Indian people.

Currently writing, Martha also designed and wrote two manuals for *Writers WordShops* and *Telling Your Story*, which she also taught. She worked as a managing editor and freelance editor, authored three books and co-authored another, wrote meditations and articles for United Methodist publications and magazines, and received the Silver Angel award from Religion in Media.

While thanking God for the luxury of writing, and especially for the privilege of getting to know Eunice Jones Mathews, Martha's favorite pastimes include her six grandchildren (ages 3–19), three children, a foster daughter and their life-partners and families. Adoring her husband Ray (for nearly fifty years now), she embraces life as pure gift. Grace is abundant . . . thanks be to God!